# Parenting
the Gifted

# SERVING SPECIAL POPULATIONS SERIES

# Parenting the Gifted

## Developing the Promise

Sheila C. Perino, Ph.D.
Joseph Perino, Ph.D.

R. R. Bowker Company
New York & London, 1981

*To the many gifted and talented children
whose stories we have told,
as well as to the parents
of these children of promise.*

Published by R. R. Bowker Company
1180 Avenue of the Americas, New York, NY 10036
Copyright © 1981 by Xerox Corporation
Printed and bound in the United States of America


**Library of Congress Cataloging in Publication Data**

Perino, Sheila C.
  Parenting the gifted.

  (Serving special populations series)
  Bibliography: p.
  Includes index.
    1. Gifted children—Identification.  2. Parenting—
United States.  3. Gifted children—Education—United
States.  I. Perino, Joseph.  II. Title.  III. Series.
HQ773.5.P43      649'.155      81-2889
ISBN 0-8352-1354-4          AACR2
ISBN 0-8352-1408-7 pbk

# Contents

# Preface

Renewed interest in the education of the gifted and talented has blossomed in recent years and there is evidence that the commitment of today's educators to these children is firm and growing. More and more states are enacting mandatory gifted education laws intended to assure long-term programs and services. *Parenting the Gifted: Developing the Promise*, a volume in Bowker's Serving Special Populations Series, is designed to fill the need for a comprehensive handbook for parents within the growing body of current literature on the gifted and talented.

Our goal in this book is to foster an understanding of gifted and talented children for you, their parents. We believe that in order to establish effective long-range programs, parents must become the partners of the professional educators. If this does not happen, today's gifted and talented movement may go the way of the enriched programs of 20 years ago, which faultered in the post-sputnik era. Toward this goal, we have sought to translate educational and technical jargon for the layperson and to provide the information and guidance necessary for parents to gain a wide perspective on the developing field of gifted and talented education. Our stance is that of parent and child advocates.

The scope of this book is the gifted child from infancy to adolescence. Emphasis is placed on child rearing, identifying the gifted and talented, understanding tests and measurements, and dealing with the schools in the promotion and selection of special programs and other educational options. One chapter is devoted to the special considerations involved in identifying and meeting the needs of atypical or "other" gifted children, including those from diverse cultural backgrounds, the female gifted, and the handicapped and learning disabled.

Additional features are a model constitution and bylaws for a parent advocacy group, a glossary of terms used in gifted and talented education, and a numbered bibliography that serves as a list of references to works discussed in the text, as well as a guide to further reading. The bibliography is divided into three levels, according to the relative difficulty and sophistication of the entries, enabling readers to advance their own education of the field at a comfortable pace. A subject index is also included.

Grateful acknowledgment is due Dr. Barbara H. Baskin, Director of the Office of Special Education at the State University of New York at Stony Brook, who not only encouraged this endeavor, but gave generously of her time, experience, and support. We are also indebted to Janet Cohen and Nancy Greggo, who worked so long and arduously on the preparation of the manuscript, and to the many parents, students, and professionals who read and offered their comments and criticism of the preliminary drafts of this work.

*Parenting the Gifted* is a culmination of our years of experience working with children and parents. We hope that it will assist you in developing your children's special gifts.

# 1
# *In the Beginning*

How did you feel when your child was identified as gifted? Surprised? Exhilarated? Confused? Apprehensive? Did you wonder if the school had the right family? One mother who was employed in an office was so sure that the principal of her son's school called only about transgressions that she took his call in a back room so that her co-workers wouldn't know! Many parents remark that they know their child is bright, but they have trouble seeing him or her as exceptional. The purpose of this book is to dispel fears, and to help you better understand your child's exceptional gifts. The book has been designed so that parents can gain a degree of familiarity with what is known concerning gifted and talented children and their educational needs. It is not intended to present citations of all the available studies in the field. However, interested readers may consult the bibliography to obtain sources of such research information for themselves.

Our intentions in writing this book are fourfold: (1) to help you learn the educational terminology; (2) to acquaint you with the available educational options; (3) to explore some concepts of personality; and (4) to suggest a variety of ways in which you can help your child to maximize his or her skills.

The parent of the gifted or talented, like the parent of the handicapped, has the enormous chore of first mastering the educational jargon. While you, the parent, are learning to "speak the language," you must also contend with the neighborhood sages. Their brand of advice tends to run anywhere from "Don't push him ahead so much" to "Have you signed her up for that special art (music) camp yet?" Even after the initial excitement dies down, you probably are left still wondering what to do next. Actually, the answer is simple—you can continue to live your regular day-to-day life, and you can stop worrying, because it is only your expectations that have changed, not your child.

It will not require a magic trick to help your child reach his or her potential. If you examine what you have already done to bring your child this far, you will probably find that, like most parents, you have already done more than you realize. Remember when the relatives were upset because you refused to use baby talk? They thought such talk was cute, but you didn't and insisted on proper grammar and ordinary words. Without knowing any sophisticated research, you were headed in the right direction. Educators have long held that talking down to children interferes with language acquisition. When you use baby talk, you are not helping your child learn to speak any more easily. In fact, you are actually asking your child to master two languages. Any child, gifted or not, will have trouble learning two different ways of communicating within a short period of time.

## Gifted or Genius? and Other Terms

Unfortunately, most of us, as adults, are far from precise in our use of words. When a teacher describes a child as "bright," we, as psychologists, do not assume that he or she is thinking of a gifted child. A bright child to the teacher is usually a youngster who is average. The description of bright connotes "not slow." What the teacher generally means is that the child comprehends, remembers facts, and generally copes well with academic tasks with no more than the usual amount of instruction time. On the other hand, we non-teachers think of bright as connoting better-than-average performance. The child may not always produce well in the classroom, but if you were to stop and talk to him or her, you would see alertness, quick insights and other advanced skills.

In the same way, popular magazine articles often describe certain children as possessing a "genius" IQ. There is no such thing. Many people believe that the words "gifted" and "genius" are synonymous, and use them interchangeably. While there is a continuing debate over the precise definition of giftedness, most experts would agree that giftedness refers to an individual's *potential* to make outstanding contributions. Genius, on the other hand, implies that the person has already produced accomplishments of lasting social value, such as a book or a symphony.

A third term that often gets jumbled in with the other two is precocious. Precocious merely refers to something that happens in advance of when you would normally expect it to occur. A person can be described as both gifted and precocious. A genius's early work may likewise be described as precocious.

Just as likely, your child may have been described as an able learner. Ruth Lawless, in *A Guide for Educating a Gifted Child in Your Classroom* (20) indicates that this label usually refers to children who are among the top performers in a given grade. Able learners frequently spell well, write neatly, and perform as would be expected when they are in school. Unfortunately, not all able learners are gifted, just as not all gifted children are able learners.

From this it is evident that labels are at best inaccurate things. Though we must all use them at times, it is best to limit their use; when you are forced to choose a label, try to use the most accurate one available.

## Gifted, Talented, and Creative

If you are looking for a clear definition of gifted, you may feel like Diogenes searching the world for an honest man. Most definitions that are available seem to focus on uniformities in gifted individuals rather than differences. The best generalization that can be made about gifted and talented children is that they usually differ somewhat less from each other than they do from the balance of the population. The 1972 Department of Health, Education, and Welfare (H.E.W.) guidelines on the education of the gifted—also known as the Marland Study (86)—talked about

*[children with] demonstrated achievement (the able learner) and/or potential in the following areas:*

1. *General intellectual ability*
2. *Specific academic talent*
3. *Creative or productive thinking*
4. *Leadership ability*
5. *Visual and performing arts*
6. *Psychomotor ability.*

According to the guidelines, a gifted or talented child may qualify under one or several of these categories. (However, during the last several years there has been some tendency to ignore psychomotor ability because schools already are attending to this area with sports programming.) Common usage in the eighties seems to imply that *gifted* indicates "general intellectual ability" and "creative or productive thinking" while *talented* refers to all the other headings from the guidelines. For the benefit of continuity, we will continue to use "gifted" and "talented" in these meanings throughout the book.

Definitions, as we have said, are often arbitrary, especially when the word to be defined is abstract and difficult to assess. The problem is worse when experts cannot agree on which label is the proper one to use. The definitions that follow are our arbitrary selections. They are composed from a variety of sources, and do not reflect any one person's point of view. It is useful to remember that a definition is like an average—it helps us better understand the overall characteristics of a group; but it does not necessarily portray with great accuracy any one individual in the group.

*Gifted children* are adept at verbal conceptualization where ideas are linked together—what is often referred to as generalization. Many of their skills produce remarkable school performance, so that they are frequently also called "the academically talented." At times you may hear this group called "left hemisphere" gifted. That label refers to the belief of scientists that abstract thinking skills, particularly verbal ones, are controlled by the left side of the brain. Gifted children are many times the ones who score most highly on traditional intelligence (IQ) tests. Educators can be fooled by these tests, however, because gifted children who come from deprived environments or who have rejected the system may not test or perform well in the classroom. All children say clever and insightful things. What distinguishes gifted children is that they say them more often, with greater depth and with more extensive elaboration.

*Creative children* have a way of going beyond set limits in thinking. They seem continually to be saying "What if?" They like to be the originators and developers of ideas. They are not put off by the unorthodox. For example, a gifted class was assigned the topics myths, legends, folklore, and other tales. They were told they could do anything with the topic they chose. Many wrote myths, some carved clay figures of the gods, and some researched cross-cultural ties. One very creative, enterprising boy devised an advertising campaign for the "Neptune" school of yachting. You can easily see how unexpected his idea was.

Experts are no more at ease when they are describing *talented children*. Some classic areas in which talent is displayed are art, music, drama, dance, writing, and sports. For many years a professional in the field was considered the best judge of a child's abilities. Today, evaluation criteria in these areas of talent are little improved, and the professional is still the best judge. However, the definition of talented seems to have broadened to include those children who have a specific academic skill or who show strength in mechanical or interpersonal areas. Talented children perform well above age expectations in these areas. They also seem to learn needed skills more quickly, even when prior exposure is lacking. Two boys will serve as good illustrations of such rapid mastery.

Alan began the violin in the fall of his fourth-grade year and in a week had mastered the first ten pages of the music book completely on his own. Within three weeks, he was a part of the orchestra and that December played in the holiday concert, something almost unheard of for a child just starting on an instrument. Alan's teacher remarked that he could discuss the physics involved and apply that knowledge to mastering the violin. The other boy, Robert, was playing three different instruments at age nine. Though he was not equally competent on all of them, he was also one of only a few fourth graders to be selected to participate in the fifth- and sixth-grade music festival.

# Individual Differences

The differences between gifted siblings can be very marked. You may have been surprised that one of your children was identified as gifted rather than another. One parent recently remarked that she never guessed that either of her children was gifted, because they had developed so much alike. It took her some time to realize that even for these very similar siblings, there were still many contrasts. One walked at six months and the other at eight months. One talked, as his mother reported, "from the womb," while his sister was not as chatty. She is more adept at math and he has a larger vocabulary. These contrasts between abilities in various children are what psychologists call "individual differences." Individual differences even in one child's abilities can be dramatic, as in the case of a child who had highly developed verbal skills but little ability to write accurately, draw, or duplicate designs.

In order to illustrate the concept of individual differences, let us discuss three siblings. David, Glen, and Marion are all gifted or talented youths. Each, however, is very different from the others. What their parents expect from one of these youngsters is not always an appropriate expectation for either of the other two. We asked their parents to go through their baby books to give us information about their early years. The following profiles are typical descriptions of how David, Glen, and Marion appear on a day-to-day basis.

## David

David was the firstborn child. As an infant, his motor skills— such as grasping, sitting alone, and walking—were fairly average. David sat alone at 7 months, walked at one year and by 16 months was described as "climbing on everything." Likewise, his language development was unremarkable. David had the usual simple word vocabulary at 14 months and by 20 months had begun to speak in sentences.

Thus, until David became a toddler, there was little to distinguish him from the average, normally developing youngster. He began to exhibit advanced behavior once he had mastered basic walking, talking, and manipulative skills. His mother noted that he had a very long attention span. At two years and ten months he began to build sophisticated structures of life-like buildings and complex geometric patterns. He was extremely curious and became knowledgeable on numerous subjects before the age of three. His parents were astounded by his logical thinking and precocious questions.

David's personality was very assertive. He never liked to do things by rote or when people told him to. He refused to take directions. While he could be productively involved in tasks of his own choosing, he resisted any attempt by his mother to teach him anything by rote, such as the alphabet. When he was four years and nine months old, David went to kindergarten. It was a large class, with almost 40 children, and David did not fit in. He was a nonconformist, and refused to participate in many activities. He had shown no preschool interest in reading, and while his readiness skills were excellent, his first school experience was not especially successful.

David's erratic school performance continued in the early elementary grades. Finally, his parents and teacher decided to have a psychological evaluation administered. While it was obvious that David was very bright, neither his parents nor the school was prepared for an IQ of 160 on the Stanford-Binet, L-M (an individual intelligence measure)—such a score occurs only once in every 10,000 cases.

Throughout elementary school, David's performance was inconsistent. He developed into an avid reader, but his motivation for academic tasks was poor. By high school, he showed a superior performance on all standardized tests, and a decided artistic ability. He still did not complete many academic tasks, and had what his parents described as a "moderate to poor self-image." His parents felt he had some athletic ability, but he treated team sports in high school much the same way he dealt with school work.

It is only now in his third year of college that David is beginning to achieve well, or to be concerned about the level of his performance. Despite his extraordinary potential, it has taken him many years to come to terms with his abilities and talents.

### Glen

David's brother Glen is some five years younger. His motor development as an infant was more erratic than David's. He grasped objects early and was only seven months old when he could crawl with great dexterity, but he learned to sit and walk at only fairly average points in his development.

What was remarkable about Glen was his response to people and his language skills, which were considerably advanced. He smiled in response to people when he was barely over 1 month old. Before 11 months, he used many words and by 16 months could speak in well-developed sentences.

Glen's disposition was very different from his brother's. He was a placid, easy-going baby, who was very attached to his mother. He developed considerable independence as well, however, and unlike his brother seemed able to cope with obstacles.

While Glen also did not read prior to attending school, he rapidly developed these skills once he was enrolled. By third grade he was an assertive child who performed consistently at an advanced level. He appeared to be a child of many talents—he was artistic, musical, and athletic, besides being a superior student.

Unlike his brother, Glen is a "team" person who enjoys having a large number of friends. He is a leader with a positive self-image and excellent social skills. Although he is still in high school, Glen's performance suggests that he will probably surpass his brother. Intellectual testing showed a performance at a slightly lower point than David's score (a score that places Glen's performance at about 1 in 1,000). However, the difference is meaningless, because Glen utilizes every scrap of his ability and thus functions far better than David does.

### Marion

Marion is about three years younger than Glen. Her motor skills were quite advanced, and she sat and walked much earlier than her brothers. Her mother describes her as very agile and physically adept at an early age. Marion exhibited excellent dexterity and like David was able to build complex structures of blocks and Lincoln logs as a toddler. She was very patient and determined when working with complicated puzzles. As she grew older, it became apparent that she understood the principles involved in the workings of mechanical things. While still in elementary school, Marion was developing her own business of repairing neighborhood bicycles.

Marion's mother noted that she did not evidence advanced verbal skills, and was in fact considerably slower in this area than either of her brothers. She was not interested in reading before she started school, and to this day is reluctant to read on her own.

While Marion was clearly at the top of her class throughout elementary school, she did not exhibit the academic facility of Glen. She was, however, a responsible child who, unlike her oldest brother, wanted to do well. Of the three children, Marion was the only one who had an opportunity to participate in a program for gifted and talented children. Her IQ score was a "modest" 130, but she demonstrated superior nonlanguage skills, especially in math and science. Marion had a gift in social areas as well and her perceptions and judgments about people were often as sophisticated as those of an adult.

Marion has athletic prowess, and participates in many sports. Her skills were good enough to make her the top basketball player in her elementary school during the sixth grade, whether she was competing with boys or with girls. Today, in junior high school, she continues to be an excellent student. Like Glen, she is motivated and responsible, and should go on to a highly productive college career.

As you can see, these youths are all very different from each other. While they all shared very superior ability, the individual differences in their styles, skills, and personalities were quite apparent from infancy. Such individual differences are what make each of us unique.

Parent handbooks frequently shrug off individual differences as inconsequential. They suggest that such differences are unimportant in the early years, and that they eventually even out and disappear. In contrast, we believe that individual differences are important and should be encouraged. After all, if everyone were the same, no one would ever have an original thought. It is true that skills are like muscles; they will atrophy if not exercised. Individual differences can be lost to a degree if not recognized early and encouraged. It would be useful for parents to take note of a child's individual differences from an early age, so that they can establish a pattern for predicting his or her later behavior.

## The Typical Child

You will often hear educators refer to the typical gifted child. The word "typical," like "average" and "normal," refers to a mathematical, or, more properly, a statistical concept. Typical characteristics are those that occur together more frequently than might be expected by chance alone.

The gifted or talented child exhibits advanced growth in his areas of skill. You can tell if the performance is advanced only if you have something to evaluate it against. This level of performance is sometimes called a "norm." Norms are obtained by comparing the test scores of one person against the scores of other individuals of similar age, social class, and other factors. (For certain skills, comparison is made only against children of the same sex, because boys and girls seem to develop at different rates for different skills, especially when they are very young.) When enough samples have been compared, a set of common characteristics—or a performance level—is derived, which psychologists call the norm. All well-developed tests have these established norms.

Once the norm has been established, it is possible to determine the degree of superiority or inferiority of a given performance. The ability of a test to make this kind of accurate discrimination depends in part on how well the norm was developed. The scores on the test are also affected by the characteristics of the tester and the motivation of the person taking the test. You should remember as well that the norm applies only to the set of skills actually measured and to the individuals from whom the norm samples were gathered. In most cases in refers to the common or most frequent performance and not to an ideal or perfect one. (See Chapter 3 for a detailed discussion of tests and scores.) The performance of the typical gifted or talented child frequently exceeds age and grade norms. Your gifted child is probably performing certain skills that are usually expected of an older child.

## One in a Million

You may be just beginning to be aware of how different your child's behaviors and skills really are. How well you understand these differences has nothing whatever to do with your own level of schooling. The highly educated mother of a gifted girl asked if her daughter truly belonged in a special program; despite the mother's education, she was unsure whether the child's performance was notably different from that of others. The word "different" in this sense refers to the idea of infrequency. How different a gifted child is depends on how infrequently the gifts occur in the total population. Different in this sense is a measure of the presence of talent or giftedness in a given child.

Let us use IQ test scores as one example. In her book *Gifted and Talented: Practical Programming for Teachers and Principals* (57), Dorothy Syphers uses the following chart to illustrate the infrequency of different IQ levels. The chart estimates how the scores might be distributed in a typical community.

| IQ Level | Number of Pupils |
|----------|------------------|
| 130 | 3 per 100 |
| 137 | 1 per 100 |
| 150 | 1 per 1,000 |
| 160 | 1 per 10,000 |
| 168 | 1 per 100,000 |
| 180 | 1 per 1,000,000 |

The mother described a child whose performance may have occurred only once in every 1,000 pupils. Her performance was certainly not a typical one.

You will often hear school personnel talking about the 3 or 5 percent participation level. They are referring to the number—3–5 percent of a school's population—that are estimated to be gifted or talented. For example, in a school with 1,000 pupils, the 3 percent participation level refers to about 30 children who are gifted; 5 percent participation level is about 50 children. In recent years there has been considerable agrument that a 3–5 percent estimate is too small, and that there really are more gifted and talented children than we first believed. Some people argue that the level is really as high as 8–10 percent of the school population. Other people have recommended throwing out a rigid percentage, and dealing with the children on a case-by-case basis, regardless of the numbers involved. Chances are your school is still using some estimate of frequency to determine how many pupils they should be servicing in gifted and talented programs. Financial considerations generally have kept most districts to the more conservative 3 percent participation level. This does not mean that the 3 percent participating in a program are the school's only gifted and talented children, but rather that this 3 percent is all the school can afford to identify and provide services for.

## Living with Being Different

In the usual course of events you can see that a gifted and talented child will be unlikely to meet others of similar abilities very often. This problem becomes greater as the degree of his or her exceptionality increases. One very real difficulty for such children is the feeling of isolation they may develop. While they can and will do many activities with their agemates, they have a definite need to cultivate friendships with children who think as they do and are interested in the same things. This need to share interests is one reason that special programs are being developed for gifted children.

The need for such special groups may seem less unusual if you consider that people join groups all the time. If you are intrigued by baseball, you may join a local team. You do this because you share with the other participants interests such as the game's strategy or a desire for exercise. Gifted children need to work with other gifted children. When this is not possible, they often either withdraw into their own isolated pursuits or submerge their skills to gain acceptance. Gifted children need to seek out challenges; when they cannot do so, they may be subject to intense frustration. As a parent, you should encourage your child to become involved in groups devoted to one of the child's specific pastimes, such as collecting old comics or rocks. Placing your child in these situations is more likely to increase his or her chances of meeting others with similar interests.

## Summing Up

Throughout the book, we will use this "summing up" section to recap the major points discussed in each chapter. This introductory section of the book was designed to whet your appetite and to stimulate your thinking about the area of gifted and talented education. We have touched on various topics and plan to clarify and elaborate on them as we proceed.

We hope this book will help you look at your child from a new and different perspective. We feel that this new way of seeing your child will assist you in understanding how others, such as the schools, are viewing him or her. It is meant to help you do the most you can to develop your child's abilities.

Gifted and talented children are not new to the world, having been around since the dawn of humankind. However, like any other natural phenomenon, they don't exist as a group until someone classifies them scientifically. So it is that around 1970 gifted and talented children were "rediscovered," and that since then specialists have been studying them and exploring the myriad ways in which they think. As parents you are in the unique and enviable position of being front-line participants in this endeavor.

# 2
# *Where the Promise Begins: The Preschool Years*

*To see a world in a grain of sand ...*
WILLIAM BLAKE

A sk most parents about their new baby and you will be treated to a three-hour monologue. They are sure that each smile and coo is not only remarkable, but suggestive of very high intellectual ability. If you have ever been trapped at a party with someone whose infant is similar in age to your own, you'll know what we mean. It can be emotionally draining to go through a session of "My baby is smarter than yours."

Making comparisons between any two children is a risky business at best. Do not try to ignore individual differences; they do exist, and not just in the minds of child psychologists! From the moment of conception children differ in the quality of the nervous system inherited. The emotional and physical health of the mother begins to interact with the child's maturation process almost immediately. This interaction is the reason physicians are so cautious about the use of medication during pregnancy and at the time of birth. It is also why pregnant women are closely monitored for a variety of pathological conditions that could contribute to physical and intellectual deficits. Women are not only becoming increasingly alert to general health warnings, but are asking their obstetricians for more precise information concerning gestation. In addition, the movement toward prepared child-birth, with its associated lower use of drugs, seems to have produced more responsive babies than those of a decade or so ago. Babies who are vigorous and responsive immediately after birth (as measured on the physician's APGAR score) seem to get off to a good start in life. Not only specific health issues, but diet and attitude contribute to your child's basic learning ability. Adages such as "You are what you eat" and "Think happy thoughts" may contain more truth than you might believe.

# Sex Differences

The innate variations in individual temperament are evident from within days of birth. Characteristics such as activity level and responsiveness have a great enough range to be measured. Researchers frequently use the word "significant" when they talk about measuring behavior. A significant event or characteristic is one that occurs more often than one would expect by chance alone.

While the evidence is still inconclusive, there is some data suggesting that girls and boys manifest different styles of learning from the first months after birth. Newborn boys seem to be significantly more active than newborn girls. Research indicates that boys, as a group, may learn best through gross motor skills, while girls learn through fine motor skills. When language development is assessed girls appear to speak sooner, with more accuracy and more often. These variations in style should not be construed as a difference in overall intelligence. The sexes are not significantly different in intelligence, but they may process information in dissimilar ways. Diane McGuinness in "How Schools Discriminate against Boys" (46), states:

*Male competency is generally displayed through the gross motor system, where it becomes coupled to three dimensional space. Female competency, on the other hand, shows through the fine motor system, where it is coordinated with audition [hearing] and visual imagery for two dimensional space.*

This research indicates that it is foolish to start comparing the accomplishments of a five-month old girl with those of a five-month old boy.

# Developmental Charts

Admonitions about making comparisons aside, you can obtain a general idea of an individual's rate of development by looking at a model of the "typical" child.

*Motor Skills*
*Sits (unsupported): 28–36 weeks*
*Stands (holding on, e.g., to furniture): approx. 36 weeks*
*Walks (unaided): 13 months*

*Language Skills*
*First word (meaningful): 44–48 weeks*
*Several words: 1 year*
*Two-word phrases: 21–24 months*

The following set of tables for examining normal and advanced developmental guidelines was constructed by Eleanor Hall and Nancy Skinner at Columbia University in New York. Note the authors' instructions for using the guidelines.

*Developmental Guidelines**
*The following developmental guidelines for normal average children were compiled from a variety of developmental timetables, including the Bayley Scales of Infant Development, the Gesell Developmental Schedules and the Slosson Intelligence Test. Your child need not be advanced in all areas to be considered gifted. However, if your child is about 30 percent more advanced than average on most items in at least one section of the table—in general motor ability, fine motor ability, or cognitive language—there is reason to believe that he or she may be gifted or talented. For example, if an average child sits up alone at seven months,*

*a child 30 percent more advanced would do so 2.10 months earlier (7 mos. × .30 = 2.10 mos.) or at 4.9 months of age (7 mos. − 2.1 mos. = 4.9 mos.)*

| General Motor Ability | Normal Months | 30% More Advanced |
|---|---|---|
| Lifts chin up when lying stomach down | 1 | 0.7 |
| Holds up both head and chest | 2 | 1.4 |
| Rolls over | 3 | 2.1 |
| Sits up with support | 4 | 2.8 |
| Sits alone | 7 | 4.9 |
| Stands with help | 8 | 5.6 |
| Stands holding on | 9 | 6.3 |
| Creeps | 11 | 7.7 |
| Stands alone well | 11 | 7.7 |
| Walks alone | 12.5 | 8.75 |
| Walks; creeping is discarded | 15 | 10.5 |
| Creeps up stairs | 15 | 10.5 |
| Walks up stairs | 18 | 12.6 |
| Seats self in chair | 18 | 12.6 |
| Turns pages of book | 18 | 12.6 |
| Walks down stairs one hand held | 21 | 14.7 |
| Walks up stairs holds rail | 21 | 14.7 |
| Runs well, no falling | 24 | 16.8 |
| Walks up and down stairs alone | 24 | 16.8 |
| Walks on tiptoe | 30 | 21.0 |
| Jumps with both feet | 30 | 21.0 |
| Alternates feet when walking up stairs | 36 | 25.2 |
| Jumps from bottom step | 36 | 25.2 |
| Rides tricycle using pedals | 36 | 25.2 |
| Skips on one foot only | 48 | 33.6 |
| Throws ball | 48 | 33.6 |
| Skips, alternating feet | 60 | 42.0 |

| Fine Motor Ability | Normal Months | 30% More Advanced |
|---|---|---|
| Grasps handle of spoon but lets go quickly | 1 | 0.7 |
| Vertical eye coordination | 1 | 0.7 |
| Plays with rattle | 3 | 2.1 |
| Manipulates a ball, is interested in detail | 6 | 4.2 |
| Pulls string adaptively | 7 | 4.9 |

| Fine Motor Ability | Normal Months | 30% More Advanced |
|---|---|---|
| Shows hand preference | 8 | 5.6 |
| Holds object between fingers and thumb | 9 | 6.3 |
| Holds crayon adaptively | 11 | 7.7 |
| Pushes car alone | 11 | 7.7 |
| Scribbles spontaneously | 13 | 9.1 |
| Drawing imitates stroke | 15 | 10.5 |
| Folds paper once imitatively | 21 | 14.7 |
| Drawing imitates V stroke and circular stroke | 24 | 16.8 |
| Imitates V and H strokes | 30 | 21.0 |
| Imitates bridge with blocks | 36 | 25.2 |
| Draws person with two parts | 48 | 33.6 |
| Draws unmistakable person with body | 60 | 42.0 |
| Copies triangle | 60 | 42.0 |
| Draws person with neck, hands, clothes | 72 | 50.4 |

| Cognitive Language | Normal Months | 30% More Advanced |
|---|---|---|
| Social smile at people | 1.5 | 1.05 |
| Vocalizes four times or more | 1.6 | 1.12 |
| Visually recognizes mother | 2 | 1.4 |
| Searches with eyes for sound | 2.2 | 1.54 |
| Vocalizes two different sounds | 2.3 | 1.61 |
| Vocalizes four different syllables | 7 | 4.9 |
| Says "da-da" or equivalent | 7.9 | 5.53 |
| Responds to name, no-no | 9 | 6.3 |
| Looks at pictures in book | 10 | 7.0 |
| Jabbers expressively | 12 | 8.4 |
| Imitates words | 12.5 | 8.75 |
| Has speaking vocabulary of three words (other than ma-ma and da-da | 14 | 9.8 |
| Has vocabulary of 4–6 words including names | 15 | 10.5 |
| Points to one named body part | 17 | 11.9 |
| Names one object ("What is this?") | 17.8 | 12.46 |

| Cognitive Language | Normal Months | 30% More Advanced |
|---|---|---|
| Follows direction to put object in chair | 17.8 | 12.46 |
| Has vocabulary of 10 words | 18 | 12.6 |
| Has vocabulary of 20 words | 21 | 14.7 |
| Combines two or three words spontaneously | 21 | 14.7 |
| Jargon is discarded, 3 word sentences | 24 | 16.8 |
| Uses I, me, you | 24 | 16.8 |
| Names three or more objects on a picture | 24 | 16.8 |
| Is able to identify 5 or more objects | 24 | 16.8 |
| Gives full name | 30 | 21.0 |
| Names 5 objects on a picture | 30 | 21.0 |
| Identifies 7 objects | 30 | 21.0 |
| Is able to tell what various objects are used for | 30 | 21.0 |
| Counts (enumerates) objects to three | 36 | 25.2 |
| Identifies the sexes | 36 | 25.2 |

Gifted children frequently achieve developmental milestones sooner than their peers. However, if your child did not seem exceptional in these early skills, you should not assume that his or her abilities are lower than those of another gifted child. R.L. Cox studied the backgrounds of 456 children and adolescents who participated in a summer program for the gifted between 1972 and 1975. The following two charts summarize the findings for walking and talking.

### Age at Which Subjects Began to Walk*

| Age (months) | Number of Children | % of Subjects |
|---|---|---|
| 6–8 | 22 | 4.8 |
| 9–11 | 246 | 53.9 |
| 12–14 | 168 | 36.8 |
| 15+ | 20 | 4.4 |

*Adapted from R. L. Cox, "Background Characteristics of 456 Gifted Children." Reprinted by permission from the *Gifted Child Quarterly* 21, no. 2 (1977): 264.

### Age at Which Subjects Began to Speak*

| Age (months) | Number of Children | % of Subjects |
|---|---|---|
| 4–6 | 34 | 9.0 |
| 7–9 | 28 | 7.4 |
| 10–12 | 174 | 46.3 |
| 13–15 | 45 | 12.0 |
| 16–18 | 56 | 14.9 |
| 19–21 | 14 | 3.7 |
| 24+ | 25 | 6.6 |
| Uncertain/NR | 80 | — |

*Adapted from R. L. Cox, "Background Characteristics of 456 Gifted Children." Reprinted by permission from the *Gifted Child Quarterly* 21, no. 2(1977): 264.

What the charts do not indicate is that the child who walked (or talked) early may have been average or late in the other skill. Only a very small percentage of children are so even in development that most of their skills are exceptionally advanced at an early age. Again, because speech seems to develop faster in girls, a gifted girl may often talk sooner and more accurately than a gifted boy. Similarly, a sex discrepancy in gross motor skills, which tends to favor boys, may be somewhat accentuated in a given child. One example of such uneven skill development is seen in a child named Michael Grost, whose overall ability level is considered to be rarer than one in a million. His mother, Audrey, remarked in her book *Genius in Residence* (13) that Michael was not a precocious talker. She pictures him scribbling furiously. "As Mike displayed neither the desire nor the intent to talk," she writes, "we wondered if he planned on writing us a letter." Michael was 19 months old when he started to talk and then he expressed himself in full sentences, not single words! While Michael Grost is certainly not the typical gifted child, his case serves to illustrate a point. Parents should not become worried that a child's skills are developing unevenly unless the delay is very marked.

As a general rule, parents of gifted children should ignore age norm charts in order to allow their children to develop at their own pace. It is of absolutely no benefit to try to push a child beyond his or her current level of readiness. Also to be avoided is the other extreme, that of placing impediments to the child's progress. Are you the parent who recalls the well-meant advice of neighbors on discouraging your early walker because "he'll only be a nuisance and get into trouble?" The two best pieces of advice for parents of bright infants are: (1) support and stimulate the child without excessive demands, and (2) don't try to block the child's unique developmental pattern by discouraging ordinary exploration of the environment. Be careful of the child's safety, but not overprotective.

In order to give you a developmental picture of a young gifted child, we'll examine the case of Laura. Much of the information we have about her early childhood comes from the baby book her mother kept carefully throughout her first years. If you suspect your child is exceptional and wish to have a record of his or her development, do not assume that you will be able to remember all the early accomplishments. Write down as much as you can—indeed about the progress of all your children. Be sure to note any behavior that strikes you as unusual. You may be glad you did later on.

Laura is the second of two children. Her brother, Alan, is some three years older. Laura was a calm, pliable infant, but active and agile. One day when she was barely six months old, Laura simply got up and ran. Her mother recalls this event quite vividly. Laura was not as verbally precocious as Alan although she knew many words by 8 months of age. She used well-developed sentences before she was 18 months old. Her mother pictured her as inquisitive and alert as a toddler. She was able to tell time by her third birthday, and had a basic sight vocabulary in reading by 2½ years.

When Laura was three, Alan was six and in first grade. The family remembers that he was just doing simple addition. For some time, Laura watched both Alan and the process with great interest. She then proceeded to master addition and subtraction on her own. By the time Laura herself was in first grade, she was multiplying three-digit numbers.

Laura's mother states that her daughter took joy in creating "something from nothing." While Alan liked to build with ready-made materials, Laura wanted to make the component parts themselves. She was not yet five when she designed patterns for doll clothes, cut them out, and then sewed the garments. Laura was obviously both highly creative and capable of advanced learning as a very young child. Her development was well beyond expectations.

## Learning Styles

If you are the parent of a preschool gifted child, of whatever age, you will need to watch and listen carefully to become familiar with his or her style of learning. One of the first things you may see is that the child is very alert and observant. From early infancy many gifted children appear to be more involved than usual in what is going on around them. This does not mean that they are necessarily physically active in their participation. Do you remember your child lying quietly in a carrier seat, his or her eyes intently following your every movement? Did you sometimes feel your child was watching you with such intensity that it was almost uncomfortable? Did you feel that he or she was storing away observations for future reference? Such alertness and intense interest in the world is considered a hallmark of the gifted child.

## Abstract Language

If your child was a precocious talker, you may have noticed that he or she initially made more complex and frequent sounds than would normally be predicted. Many gifted children are intrigued with words and language from an early point in time. They use complex phrases and sentences while others are barely beyond the da-da, ma-ma babbling phase. They generally have a knack for systematically putting one right word after another. Such organization of language in itself means nothing if the child does not understand what he or she is saying. But gifted children do more than merely ape the way their elders speak. They possess a quick and thorough grasp of abstract concepts. A good example of such a preschooler was the boy who was asked to tell how gasoline and kerosene are similar. He responded, "I know you want me to say that they're combustible substances, but I prefer to say that they are hydrocarbon compounds." Of course, this is not the response of the most typical gifted child, but it reflects the type of insight gifted children can be expected to exhibit.

Gifted children are able to see past the obvious answer, often giving sophisticated responses to questions. Sometimes this elaboration causes them problems, since they may give more information than the questioner intended or desired. It can even lead them occasionally to the wrong answer. Take, for example, the boy who was asked why gasoline floated on water. He answered that the gasoline was lighter than the water it displaced. Of course, he was wrong, because there is no displacement involved when gasoline floats on water.

Thinking in the abstract means the ability to sort, classify, compare, and contrast things or ideas by characteristics or function. One key to such abstract thinking is flexibility. Flexible thinkers are able to shift their method of concept sorting at will in order to look at the same information in a different way. Flexible thinkers are risk takers. They are more willing to guess when the need arises. They do not resist tackling unusual projects because to them no task is unique; they always find something from past experience to aid them in dealing with the current situation.

## Vocabulary

Along with skill in manipulating abstract concepts your verbally gifted child will often exhibit advanced vocabulary. In examining vocabulary, we can break it down into two types, called receptive and expressive.

Receptive vocabulary refers to the type of words your child can understand, but may not necessarily be able to explain or use in daily speech. Gifted children tend to understand or comprehend more words than the typical child their age. You probably found at an early juncture that your child could follow complicated directions and appeared to "know" a remarkable number of objects and places by name. This connection between the sounds of a language and the labels or names of objects, places, actions, or qualities is part of receptive vocabulary. The other half of receptive vocabulary is associating the label with the abstract meaning of the word.

Expressive vocabulary refers to words your child can explain and may frequently use in everyday speech. Expressive vocabulary is one of a child's verbal skills that you will be most likely to notice. For example, verbally gifted children are more likely to define a lemon as a citrus fruit than as something to eat. Their speech is colorful because of the large number of adjectives they include. These children are adept at giving synonyms, and they also demonstrate advanced labeling skills. (Labeling simply means calling a thing by its name.)

Just as verbally gifted children tend to understand more

labels, they are also more apt to use more accurate words. They are likely to name something explicitly rather than saying "it" or "that thing." An example of this type of child was a five-year-old with a consuming interest in rocks and minerals. Prior to visiting a lapidary, he spent hours looking at small samples in his collection so that he could be familiar with their names. You can well imagine the proprietor's amazement when the boy rushed up to an immense specimen happily shouting, "Oh, look at the beautiful quartz crystal!" This type of vocabulary, which you may be tempted to consider "fancy" words, is likely to characterize the speech of the verbally gifted child. Teachers of the gifted become accustomed to children such as the fourth-grade girl who refers to cows as bovines, or the first-grade explorer of science who discourses on control variables. Verbally gifted children are great collectors of words. They collect words as they collect nearly everything else, with vigor and attention to detail. Their determination is often compulsive and extends over a long period of time.

## Motor Skills

While young verbally gifted children seem determined to master their world, you should be aware that manual dexterity is not always one of their strong points. However, it is fortunate that these are skills that generally improve with practice. You can subtly encourage such practice by the types of activities and toys you select. Your child needs to cut, paste, paint, and use clay despite his or her interest in what may be considered more esoteric pursuits. Encouraging independence in self-help skills—such as dressing and feeding—also aids in developing dexterity.

Children whose strong skills are in nonverbal areas present an entirely different picture from verbally gifted children. Early proficiency in walking frequently is their trademark. They are able to grasp and hold objects accurately where other infants will not even make an effort to do so. Long before the norms would suggest, children gifted in motor skills are struggling to sit unaided and pull themselves upright. They are throwing objects farther and more accurately. Their balance is frequently superb. They are adept at reproducing long patterns of behavior they have observed. They appear to be fascinated with building complex structures from blocks and drawing endless streams of pictures. The mother of such a girl recently remarked that her daughter seemed "to be born with a crayon in her hand." These are the children who effortlessly put together puzzles and by age three may be masters of the art. They are also the children seen dragging sawed-off tennis rackets to the courts at under five, swimming several laps of a pool by a little over age two, or attempting to pick out tunes on any available musical instrument.

## The Collectors

Gifted children in general are avid collectors. They collect to such a degree that one house may have trouble storing the many examples of their multiple interests. After the first burst of interest is over, they do not necessarily discard their collections, but put them away, to resurrect them at a future date. The return of an interest is often of an intensity similar to the original obsession.

One theory about why individuals collect such diverse things as rocks and buttons, or at a later age stamps and comics, is that it is a form of conceptual sorting as suggested by such behavioral scientists as J. P. Guilford and N. K. Humphrey. A collection is not a collection unless there is very little duplication. Specimens may vary in only some fine, slight ways, but they are nonetheless different from each other. What seems to interest the collector is that the specimens are both similar and different at the same time. The objects are similar because they are in the same family or class (for example, cone shells), while they are dissimilar because of some characteristic such as size, color, or mottling. The function of such comparisons may be a way of arriving at denotative (definable) meaning. They teach the child that there are definable groupings of things or ideas. The benefit of such an abstract skill is that it helps the child make generalizations from one instance to the next. No learning experience, as mentioned previously, is unique.

## Early Reading

You can begin to see that a variety of activities may suggest an unusual level of ability in the preschool child. Still another such indicator is early reading. While precocious academic skills do not necessarily single out the gifted child, it is estimated that many gifted children read before coming to school. The beginnings of this skill are often so subtle that a parent may overlook them. One mother remembers that from less than a year of age, her son was aware when his picture books were upside down. No matter how many times this occurred, he consistently changed them back to the correct position. The parents of a multitalented girl recall similar behavior. They remarked that she always went through her books from left to right as if "reading" them. She would spend considerable time studying the page and then thoughtfully go on to the next one. Parents of such children report that either they first demonstrated reading skills by identification of single words (called sight vocabulary), or they seemed just to start reading simple sentences. In most instances the parents had done little formal instruction other than pointing out letters of the alphabet. Some early readers move quite suddenly from nonreading to reading. One little boy did not read until seven months before he started kindergarten. When he was tested shortly after school commenced, his word reading and comprehension skills ranged from fourth- to seventh-grade levels—admittedly a remarkable transformation!

The parents' reaction when they realize their child is reading is often one of disbelief. They may assume that the child is not really reading but only remembering stories that were read aloud. Initially, this may be true, but such memorization quickly passes into real reading.

How early is early? Some experts feel that as many as 50 percent of those children who will read before coming to school will do so by age 2–2½. Their initial mastery of this skill is largely self-taught. One factor educators agree on is that parental modeling of reading skills, as well as availability of reading materials in the home, has a big impact on encouraging the early reader. "My wife read to our daughter from day one," recalls one man. She did not read just stories to the child, but recipes on labels on boxes as well!

## Mathematics

Basic arithmetic skills can also appear at an early juncture. Like reading, mathematics skills begin with an understanding of underlying concepts. In reading, children learn to match the symbol with the abstract meaning of the word. In mathematics, they master ideas such as "most," "least," and "none" before they internalize the meaning of specific number symbols. Many children who will later show advanced mathematical skills exhibit an early interest in time, measurement, and simple arithmetic calculations. They are curious about the makeup and need for clocks and are prone to asking questions such as "how long," "how many," or "how much." These gifted children are fascinated with birthdays and age. They ask awkward questions such as "If Grandma is 86 years old, when is she going to die?" There also seems to be some connection between motor and perceptual development, especially in what is termed spatial ability (the ability to see things in time and space, such as direction and position), and skill at mathematics. The child who has demonstrated early motor development is somewhat more likely to also show strength in mathematics.

A child's arithmetic skills will benefit if the parent is precise in giving directions. Asking for "a can of peas" or the "biggest can of peas" instead of "the peas" encourages the child to discriminate numerical concepts. Gifted children often become intrigued with counting. Many a parent has remarked that their three-year-old loves to count to 100 over and over again. Gifted children many times master some of the basic computational operations before or during kindergarten. Whether such skill mastery will occur depends as much on the temperament of the individual child as on the amount of basic ability in mathematics that is present.

## Memory

Many gifted children seem to possess remarkable memories. This may not necessarily appear in immediate retention of instructions, but rather in what is called "long-term retrieval" of both isolated facts and complex types of information. In one sense, such children may seen to be trivia experts. They not only remember who invented what, but the inventor's middle name as well. They want to know all the details about any subject you may be discussing, even details no one else seems to care about. The gifted child is just as likely to be able to recall and organize a vast store of facts on a single topic. A perennial favorite for the preschool set is dinosaurs; many a gifted five-year-old knows more about dinosaurs than does the average adult.

## Curiosity and Persistence

Gifted preschoolers tend to be insatiably curious and ask endless questions. While they invariably ask the usual who, what, and when queries, they are frequently more interested in the why and how of things. The gifted child shows intense interest in chores that may seem to you only everyday occurrences. Suppose you are cleaning tarnish off your copper-bottomed pots or rust from the outdoor furniture. Your child not only wants to know what "that stuff" is, but how it got there and if it will come back after you clean it off. Before long, you may find yourself trying to explain oxidation and how one chemical can affect another. About this time you will be noticing how persistent your child is. If you can't answer the questions and suggest "Let's find out," you may be treated to a junket through several community libraries. If this hasn't happened to you yet, the moment may be fast approaching. One harried mother was dragged hither and yon by her fourth-grade daughter looking for material for her school project. Nothing seemed to satisfy the girl's desire for exactness. What especially exasperated the mother was that her daughter finally did the project from material she already had at home. When the daughter was asked why they had to try so many different places for the information, the reply was that she could tell if her material was adequate only after she had investigated everything on the subject.

## Energy

Hand in hand with persistence seems to go seemingly inexhaustible energy. Gifted children appear almost driven to explore their environment. They frequently are involved in so many activities that their worried parents fear they may collapse. This is less likely to occur if the child (and not the parent) is the one scheduling the child's time. More often it is the parent who will feel exhausted trying to keep up with the child's multitude of interests.

The large amounts of time spent in almost frantic activity correspond with a decrease in the amount of sleep the child seems to require. A great number of parents recall that right from the start their gifted children slept less than their brothers and sisters. These are children who rise early and generally refuse to nap during the day. As a mother remarked, "Once she's awake, she stays up." The amount of sleep an individual needs is not as predetermined as you may have believed. Parents of such a child should resist imposing naps unless the child is cranky and obviously needs the rest. The amount of sleep a child requires is another type of individual difference. Gifted children just seem to need less of it than the rest of us!

This type of frantic activity should not be confused with hyperactivity; the gifted child is clearly focused in his pursuits, while the efforts of the hyperactive child are scattered.

## Friendships

You will find that the preschool gifted child often prefers to be with older children and adults. Some educators feel it serves no productive purpose to push the child to associate with peers instead of older people. Where sophisticated play activities or special interests are involved, there is no harm in letting the child socialize with more mature individuals. At the same time, playing with peers will keep the child from becoming too "different." The best course is to play the situation by ear and try to avoid any tendency on the child's part toward total isolation.

## Summing Up

The years of the preschool period are aptly named the formative years. They are a time of inquiry and learning for all children. The gifted child must learn to master the same self-help and social skills that his peers are dealing with while at the same time coping with a variety of advanced abilities.

The preschool years are a time when you, the parent, see the first glimmers of what your child can become. He or she may dazzle you with insight, occasionally embarrass you with all too precise memory, and generally prove a challenge to

your own energy and creative skills. Help your child to become a thinker, not just a gifted information gatherer. Teach
him or her to listen, observe, and evaluate. Encourage the
child to consider the ideas of others. Do not put him or her on
display or emphasize this exceptionality—the child already
knows that he or she is different. Stimulate without pushing.
Don't set goals for your child, but do allow progress at as fast
a pace as he or she desires. Try not to dwell only on the
strengths, but also to support the child's attempts to overcome weaknesses. The parent of a gifted preschooler needs
endurance, a sense of humor, and the ability to organize both
time and space. Remember that you must provide a model of
the behavior you wish your child to show. Speak to your child
as you would like your child to speak, and encourage a love of
learning and reading. As time spans are measured, the preschool years are very short, but they are the foundation on
which your child must build a future.

# 3
# IQ Is Not Enough

*Intelligence is the ability to think*
*rationally, act purposefully and deal*
*effectively with the environment.*
DAVID WECHSLER

H ave you ever purposely sat down to think about what the term intelligence means? If so, you will not be surprised to learn that the word has many connotations. People who are not part of the psychology profession or the educational system have a very different view of intelligence from that of school personnel. Many people see common sense as a key factor in intelligence, while most educators think of intelligence as related to school performance. How often have you heard someone mutter "Brother! For a person with a college education, that was a stupid thing to do!" In point of fact, neither the professional nor the lay person is entirely right or wrong. Intelligence is made up of many factors, including both common sense and the way one performs on tests.

Intelligence is not something you can reach out and touch; it is an abstract concept, and there is no way anyone can absolutely assess it. The best psychologists and educators can do is to make an estimate. What they estimate is not what one's abilities were yesterday or what they may be ten years from now but what they are today. This type of estimate is called an assessment of *current functioning*.

# About Tests

Regardless of what talent or skill we are interested in, we need ways to measure its presence. You will hear educators bandying around terms like validity, reliability, stanine, percentile, normal curve, standard deviation, and standard error of measurement. You need not be put off by the use of these words; they are not as difficult to understand as you might think. Let's take a closer look at them and see how they may be applied to your child's performance.

You may need to read this section over several times before it becomes clear, but it will be well worth the effort. Psychologists often give people scores they don't understand, and they then misuse them. If you understand where the scores come from, you will not misuse them.

## Test Construction

When tests are constructed, those designing them realize that intelligence, achievement, and creativity are really only abstract concepts that will never be measured totally. The best that testers can hope for is to estimate the level at which a person is presently performing or functioning. This functioning level can vary because of such factors as motivation, fatigue, what aspects of the skill are being evaluated, and how well the test was constructed.

Tests are designed so that those questions that are most often answered correctly by the largest proportion of the population are considered the easiest. Likewise, those questions that are more rarely answered correctly are considered the most difficult, as noted by Anne Anastasi in *Psychological Testing* (60). A properly developed test starts with easy items and progresses to harder ones.

## How to Have a Good Test

When you are interested in children at the high extreme of an ability, the test must have a large number and variety of sufficiently difficult items if it is to measure individual differences among the different high scores. This is called having a high enough "ceiling." The same idea applies to the easy end of the test. When you do not have a large number and variety of easy items for handicapped individuals, the result is a test with an insufficient "test floor."

When norms are developed for tests, it is important that the test be predictable. That means that an individual's scores should be fairly similar, whether the person takes the test today, next week, or next year. The similarity should persist unless the person actively does something to alter the performance. This similarity of scores is called "test reliability." How different your actual scores on the test are from time to time is called the "standard error of measurement." Obviously, a better and more accurate test has good reliability and a low error of measurement. This is true of individual intelligence tests such as the Wechsler Intelligence Scale for Children–Revised (WISC-R) and the Stanford-Binet, L-M, where the variation is about five points. Where the arguments in test design get heated is over the term "validity." What a test measures, how well it does so, and for whom determines its validity. Disadvantaged minority groups frequently perform differently from middle-class groups on standard tests; the interpretation of their scores—and the validity of the tests—is therefore open to debate.

It is most important for a parent to know exactly what skills a particular test does sample. To determine this it is not enough to look only at the name of a test; its content must be examined too. You can find out more about a test by asking the school psychologist who administers the test.

## The Normal Curve

As Anastasi (60) explains, if a test has sampled a good cross section of the population, the scores from the test should fall into a pattern. This statistical pattern is called the normal curve and is illustrated in Figure 1.

If you look at the normal curve, the large bulge you see at its center is where the scores of most people in the test would fall. This section of the group or distribution would then be considered average. Infrequent and below-average performances are on the left side of the curve; infrequent and above-average performances are on the right side of the curve.

The measure called the "standard deviation" (SD) tells us how the test scores are distributed on the normal curve; it is a sort of place-mark on the curve. For example, if we had 100

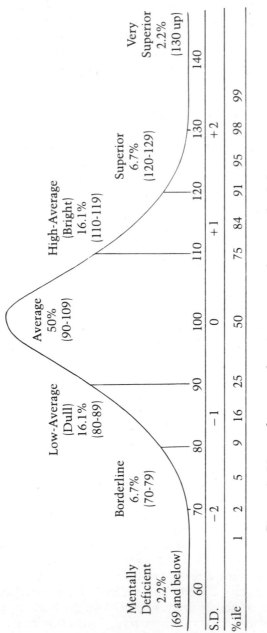

Figure 1. Normal curve, showing percentiles, standard deviations and David Wechsler's Intelligence Classifications.

people take a test, approximately 50 of them would fall in the classification called average. As a group their scores would fall on either side of the center line in the normal curve; this center is labeled the "mean." This area of average scores is referred to as a little less than one standard deviation. Another 16 persons would fall on either side of the first group and be considered either high or low average. Another 7 people will stand at the ends of the low/high average groups. One set of 7 will be considered to have obtained a superior test performance and the other a low or borderline performance. Finally, 2 or 3 people will stand at the farthest ends of the score distribution. This group's scores are two or more standard deviations from the mean. The high group has given a very superior performance and the low group a deficient performance. When psychologists tell you that your child's scores place him or her in the top 2 percent of the country for certain skills, they mean that his or her score falls at least two standard deviations from the average groups and would be marked at the high end of the distribution. The child's performance would therefore exceed that of 98 out of every 100 people.

## Percentiles and Stanines

Percentiles are another way of comparing your child's test scores to those of the rest of the children taking the test. Like the standard deviation, percentiles tell you the individual's position relative to the average performance. Percentiles start at the bottom with one for the lowest performance. It takes a certain number of correct responses on the test to obtain a higher percentile. For example, a percentile of 50 indicates that the score is higher than 49 percent of the children tested, while a percentile of 99 indicates that only 1 percent of those tested scored higher.

A third way of looking at performance is stanines. Stanines, as the name implies, are numbered from 1 to 9. The most common or average performances are labeled stanines 4, 5, or 6. This is like saying your average score is within plus or minus one standard deviation from the center of the normal curve. As you might guess, the eighth stanine is approximately between one and two standard deviations. The ninth stanine is a performance at least 1.8 standard deviations from the center of the curve. About 3 people in each group of 100 will obtain the ninth stanine on a test.

Percentiles and stanines are frequently used ways of reporting test scores on achievement tests. A stanine's most negative characteristic is that it limits your knowledge of the child's performance. Let's say Meg and John are in the fourth grade. Meg's stanine in reading is 9 and so is John's. All this says is that Meg and John are performing better than most of the children at their grade level. It does not indicate at what grade level they can actually perform—Meg might be comfortable at a fifth-grade level, for instance, and John at the top of fourth.

### The Meaning of "Significance"

Significant refers to those events or traits that occur more frequently than they would by chance alone. Usually researchers refer to a degree (or level) of significance, typically the .05 or the .01 levels. To put it simply, a .05 or .01 significance level means that in 100 instances the behavior would have happened by chance alone only 5 times (.05) or only once (.01).

When a person talks about significance levels, it's like talking about the odds in betting. If you have a finding significant at the .01 level, it is like saying that odds of the bet's being wrong by chance alone were 100 to 1. Thus, researchers use significance levels to help them determine that the events they are measuring are not merely occurring at random.

# Intelligence

### The Nature-Nurture Question

The description of intelligence is the subject of intense controversy among psychologists and educators. Theorists have been fascinated for years not only by the makeup of intelligence, but by what proportions of its character are contributed respectively by heredity and by environment—often called the controversy between nature and nurture. It is generally agreed that while the basic quality of the nervous sytem is inherited, the environment can work many changes on it. While it is not our intention to delve deeply into genetic factors or heredity patterns here, one observation needs to be made.

Test score estimates of children's innate potential are generally found to be highly related to estimates of their parents' intelligence. For example, when Harold McCurdy, in his essay

"Childhood Patterns of Genius" (84), reviewed the biographies of such eminent individuals as Goethe and John Quincy Adams, he noticed that "early promise of [these] very distinguished men can not be dissociated from the intellectual qualities evident in their parents and transmitted . . . genetically as well as socially to their offspring." McCurdy's statement is over 20 years old but recent researchers such as Kathleen Montour have supported his observations.

## Heredity

Research indicates that to some extent intelligence is controlled by heredity. Studies on identical twins—whose genetic makeup is considered identical—show that their scores on intelligence tests are similar, more similar than the scores of parents and child or of nontwin siblings. We can deduce from this that their similar biological makeup is a strong factor in the similarity of their scores.

## Environmental Factors

When we examine environmental factors in intelligence, questions arise. How many environmental variables are important? Which environmental factors have the most influence? There is no final answer to either of these questions. The chief reason for what might seem to be a case of fence-sitting by experts is the nature of research in the social sciences. Unlike such "hard" sciences as biology, in social science researchers do not talk about cause and effect. Instead they talk about something termed correlations. To put it simply, a correlation refers to the relationship between two things or events, for example, the number of books in the home and a child's IQ score. If researchers state that there is a positive correlation between these two factors, they mean that a child living in a home that contains more books tends to have a higher IQ score. What they would *not* say is that if you rush out and buy 200 books, your child's IQ score will jump noticeably. The reason the researcher will not talk about cause and effect when dealing with environmental factors is that the effects of different factors often overlap; it is difficult to identify any single factor as the cause of a given effect. Let's pursue the example of the number of books in a child's home. It might not be the books themselves that are important to the child's IQ score, but the amount of parental education, the parent's efforts to stimulate the child, the family's affluence, or maybe all these things taken together.

Even when research can clearly determine the effects of given factors, it may turn out that the effect of the number of books on the child's IQ score is only slight. The fact is that the environment is very complex. We should be careful of putting too much trust in those who claim to know just which environmental factors have a major impact on intelligence. It is too simplistic to ask whether intelligence is the result more of the environment or of heredity. The elements in each category may be extremely diverse. Intellectual functioning can reflect such factors, for example, as nutrition, medical care, and the amount of parental interest in the child's accomplishments.

J. P. Guilford, in *The Nature of Human Intelligence* (78), sums up the nature/nurture question best when he states:

*The general conclusion to be drawn from all such information, to which there is considerable agreement, is that both heredity and environment contribute conditions determining the general intellectual status of individuals as measured by intelligence tests. Both heredity and environment, to the extent that the latter is stable during the formative years, establish upper limits for development. Rarely does any individual reach either limit. The status that he achieves will be below the limit determined by either heredity or environment, whichever is lower. No statement can readily be made regarding lower limits.*

## One Factor or Many

There are two ways to view intelligence. One approach is to picture it as made up of a single, broad, unitary skill. This method suggests that we can estimate intelligence using a single score. As time has gone on, this single score has become known as the intelligence quotient of IQ score. Unfortunately, the notion of intelligence as a unitary concept has been so popular that people have often misused the information gained from testing.

An alternate approach is to say that intelligence is made up of many factors. The most prominent proponent of this approach is J. P. Guilford of the University of Southern California. Guilford has proposed that some 120 factors contribute to intelligence, although no one can perform equally well in all of these skills. The individual's unevenness produces a pattern that we call a "profile," which shows us how a person learns and suggests what might be the best approach for teaching him or her. Guilford's theory (called the Structure of Intellect, or SOI, model) is particularly useful in education of the gifted where instruction must go beyond just the transmission of factual information and correct solutions.

## IQ Tests

An IQ test, rather than testing overall intelligence, is merely one sample of a variety of behavior. It should be noted that a person's test score can be affected by factors besides intelligence—such as degree of motivation, anxiety, fatigue, and state of health. As we have discussed, test reliability is the ability of a test to predict accurately from one situation to another. A person's score on an accurate test will be quite similar to any other score he or she receives on the same test under normal circumstances. The key words in this statement are "normal circumstances" and "score." Normal circumstances implies that when you take the test you are not sick, tired, or under undue stress; the term also assumes that you want to do well and try your best. Educators call this type of effort "motivation." When you are unmotivated, overanxious, sick, or very tired, your test score will be unreliable. Furthermore, the score on an intelligence test is merely a sample that compares one person's performance on that test with that of other people of similar age. It is related to intelligence, but it is not an absolute measurement of intelligence.

### What's Wrong with IQ Scores

Most people do not realize that intelligence tests are made up of many different tasks. The IQ score is something like the average between those items on which you perform well and those items on which you perform poorly. Two children may have the same IQ score but may have achieved it in quite different ways. If we are trying to instruct these two children, it is most important to see their individual strengths and weaknesses rather than the full IQ scores, which just happened to be identical. One child may have a higher potential in mathematics than the other. Neither child's math ability may have been exercised anywhere near capacity in the past. A profile will enable us to make more realistic demands in math for each of these children. Using the IQ score in isolation leads us to demand too much in some situations and not enough in others.

Another difficulty with intelligence tests is that they sample only a few skills. For instance, only about 31 of Guilford's 120 factors are measured on WISC-R, a well-known individual test. While this seems like a small sample of skills, it is relatively high when compared with group tests or more specialized measures. This indicates that we as parents need to be more critical of tests and what we think they tell us. Intelligence tests portray only a select sample of one's abilities.

## Choosing Tasks for Intelligence Tests

The name of a Frenchman, Alfred Binet, is often associated with the origin of intelligence testing. Binet was not the first of his countrymen to have an interest in testing; he was preceded by Esquirol and Sequin. However, his name is probably best known to people outside the fields of psychology and education. In 1904, Alfred Binet was asked to identify the slow learners in the Paris schools. In response, he developed a test that was the forerunner of the present-day Stanford-Binet, L-M intelligence scale. Two important findings resulted from Binet's early work with tests. Binet discovered that testers could talk about a child's performance by saying that the child could pass (or not pass) tasks usually expected of an older or younger child. This led to the idea of "mental age" (MA), a concept retained today on the Stanford-Binet, L-M. If you were to examine the cover sheet of your child's IQ test or report, you would find a space for the child's actual age (called the chronological age—CA) and his mental age. Both ages would be stated in years and months. For example, you might see: Jane Smith, CA (chronological age) 5-4 (five years and four months); MA (mental age) 8-3 (eight years and three months). You should bear in mind that this mental age is the balance point of Jane's passes and failures on the test tasks. Not all her skills will be similar to those of a child eight years and three months old— some will be like those of a child younger than 8-3, and some like those of a child older than 8-3.

The second finding from Binet's work was that test scores can be used to predict school performance. This relationship is the reason certain tasks were represented on early intelligence tests. Binet and the Paris school officials were interested in predicting academic success, and today modern intelligence test items are still best at predicting academic progress rates. The tasks they include—which were selected for their ability to predict that progress—tend to emphasize memory, cognition (comprehension), and convergent production tasks (finding the one best right answer).

Convergent production is called by many the "school block" of skills. It is the ability to find the best right solution to problems. Mary Meeker, in *The Structure of Intellect* (91), points out that convergent ability is "almost synonymous with curriculum assimilation, 'where the emphasis is upon achieving' . . . [the] conventionally accepted best outcomes." It has been estimated that 70 percent of the school curriculum is made up of convergent-type tasks, although according to Guilford's model of intelligence, convergent tasks represent only 28 skill factors.

IQ tests are very accurate on the type of prediction for which they were designed. However, as we have already pointed out, they are less than effective in forecasting later achievement in life.

## IQ Numbers and How to Translate Them

We have already discussed the normal curve in this chapter. The estimate of the frequency of an IQ score is based on this statistical model of the normal curve. The labels or names used on intelligence tests (such as "average") were developed to identify different sections of the normal curve. Thus the top 2–3 percent, with scores of 130 or higher, is called very superior; the next highest 6 percent, with scores of 120–129, is called superior; the next 16 percent, with scores of 110–119, is called high average; and the group with scores of 90–109 is called average. Among professionals there is some minor variation in assigning classification labels to specific IQ scores, the system we use is that developed by David Wechsler, as described in his *Manual for the Wechsler Intelligence Scale for Children—Revised* (100).

## Group IQ Measures

Group IQ tests—taken by many people at one time—were developed to provide quick, relatively cheap mass screening techniques for industry, the military, and school systems. The key words here may be "quick," "cheap," and "mass." items selected for group IQ tests must, of necessity, be suited to testing with paper and pencil. A degree of reading skill is frequently required, especially at the older levels. Such tests allow for large amounts of chance guessing because of the number of "select the right answer" type of questions.

Group intelligence tests tend to be inaccurate for higher IQ scores. How inaccurate? The researcher Pegnato examined the relationship between group IQ scores and those obtained on more accurate individual measures. He found minimal correlation between the scores. An individual could score fairly poorly on the group test and still score 136 on the individual. Using a cutoff score of 120 on the group tests, 20 percent of the gifted students (who scored 136 or better on the individual tests) would not be identified as gifted. When the cutoff was dropped to 115, only 8 percent were missed. If you consider that many experts in gifted education favor a much more liberal IQ cutoff score on the individual tests (when a cutoff is used at all)—around 120 instead of 136—you can well imagine what proportion of gifted children are overlooked when mass screening techniques are used. However, group IQ tests are helpful as a coarse screening technique when (1) the bottom cutoff (lowest acceptable) group score is kept liberal; (2) individual exceptions to the cutoff group are evaluated on a case-by-case basis; and (3) all children receive an individual test prior to entrance into the program.

If your child has been tested on a group intelligence test, it is likely to have been one of the following measures:

### Preschool to Kindergarten

1. Goodenough-Harris Drawing Test. A drawing of a person is done by the child. Points are obtained for the accuracy of the figure. Fine motor deficits will not necessarily depress the score.
2. Vane Kindergarten Test. This test has three parts: a figure drawing scored similarly to the Goodenough, a vocabulary

portion, and a section where geometric shapes must be reproduced.

### Kindergarten to Twelth Grade

1. California Test of Mental Maturity. This test has five factors, dealing with memory, language, reasoning, and perceptual and mathematical ability.
2. Lorge Thorndike Intelligence Test. The kindergarten and first-grade parts are nonverbal. The other grade levels have both verbal and nonverbal sections. Skills tapped include vocabulary, classification, and relationships between words or symbols.
3. Otis Lennon Mental Ability Test and Kuhlmann-Anderson Intelligence Test. Both these tests are similar to the foregoing measures.

### Individual Intelligence Measures

Individual tests tend to be underutilized because they are costly and can be administered only by trained, qualified personnel. The additional cost for materials is not a staggering amount. Usually test kits do not need to be purchased because school districts have already bought them for assessment of the handicapped, where individual assessment is the rule and not the exception; and test score sheets are all fairly comparable in price. The cost is incurred in the professional time required to administer and score individual tests. As you can see, testing cost and the need for qualified personnel are actually one and the same issue. We will discuss the reality of this situation as well as possible solutions in Chapter 8.

Reading is not an issue in individual IQ tests. Very little material on these tests needs to be read, and for that which does, the examiner is allowed to read the questions to a child who cannot read. Individual tests have the advantage of allowing some questioning of responses, observation of test behavior, and a wider selection of the tasks presented. Obviously a child's motivation during the examination session, as well as the examiner's own testing characteristics, can affect the accuracy of test results. However, group tests are influenced by the same types of student/examiner motivational factors as are individual tests, so that the individual test's accuracy is no more affected by personality factors than is group test accuracy. Following is a description of several well-known individual intelligence tests.

*Stanford-Binet, L-M*  The Standford-Binet was designed for use with persons from age two through adulthood, and takes approximately one hour to administer. The most recent major revision of the test was in 1960, but the charts (called norm tables), from which the IQ scores are derived, were revised in 1972.

Many tasks on the Stanford-Binet, especially at the lower age levels, appeal to children because they appear to be games rather than the tests children have encountered in school. Skills are tested at age levels, such as five, six, or seven years old. Tests within each age level are considered to be of similar difficulty. An alternate test, also of similar difficulty, is provided at each age level, should one of the original level tasks be ruined (for example, by unforeseen outside distractions such as fire drills). Tasks on the Stanford-Binet are something of a smorgasbord, both within and between levels. For example, vocabulary, while tested at one level, might not be tested for two more levels. Conversely, there may be more than one vocabulary-type task on a given level.

You will sometimes see reference to a "basal" and a "ceiling" level. The basal level is the age level at which a child passes all items presented. The ceiling level is the level at which the child fails all items presented.

The Stanford-Binet places more emphasis on language skills than on nonlanguage skills. There are few time limits on tasks, and those that appear are liberal. Scoring goes as high as 160 on the norm tables; higher performance must be estimated.

The Stanford-Binet is a popular test, especially for younger children, for whom relatively few tests are available. However, like any test, it has its limitations. As Anne Anastasi (60) suggests, it is not especially suitable for adults in the superior or better range because of its low test ceiling (the number of appropriate, difficult items at those levels). The test is also slightly more reliable with children older than age five, where IQ scores of 140 or better are involved. Culturally different and poor-children's scores tend to suffer because of the tests' emphasis on language items and the type of children on which it was standardized. Findings on the Stanford-Binet are given as a mental age and an IQ score. No further breakdown of the tested areas is provided.

*Wechsler Intelligence Scale for Children—Revised (WISC-R)*
WISC-R is one of a family of tests developed by David Wechsler.* It is the 1974 revision of the original Wechsler Intelligence Scale for Children (WISC) designed by Wechsler in 1949. The WISC-R, like the Binet, takes approximately an hour to administer. It is appropriate for children from 6 years to 16 years 11 months old, and is available in Spanish as well as English.

Wechsler states that he "abandoned" the concept of mental age because it is difficult to interpret. In its place he has substituted a "deviation IQ." Using the deviation IQ method, children's scores are compared with "the scores earned by individuals in a single [that is, his or her own] age group." Thus, if your child is 8 years and 8 months old, his or her scores will be compared only with those of children between 8 years, 8 months, and 0 days old and 8 years, 11 months, and 30 days old.

The WISC-R is divided into two halves, a verbal section, which is mostly untimed, and a performance section, which is completely timed. The verbal tasks are information, similarities, arithmetic, vocabulary, comprehension, and digit span. The performance tasks are picture completion, picture arrangement, block design, object assembly, coding (A or B form), and mazes. Frequently digit span and mazes are not given under normal circumstances. These two tests often serve the purpose of alternate (or substitute) tasks for their sections of the WISC-R just like the alternates on the Binet. If they are given as part of the regular test, their scores are not counted in the IQ computations. Three IQ scores are provided: verbal, performance, and full. The full score reflects the combination of the verbal and performance sections.

You will frequently hear reference to "scaled scores." The scaled score is a number that stands for the comparison of a child's performance with that of the age peer group. Scaled scores range from 1 to 19, with scores of 15 or better equivalent to a very superior performance.

While scores on WISC-R and the Stanford-Binet tend to be similar for a given child, the Stanford-Binet score may tend to be more similar to the WISC-R verbal score alone rather than to the full IQ score. Like the Binet, WISC-R suffers from diffi-

*The following material is from David Wechsler, *Manual for the Wechsler Intelligence Scale for Children—Revised* (New York: The Psychological Corporation, 1974). Copyright © 1974 by the Psychological Corporation. By permission of The Psychological Corporation.

culty in measuring the highest scores. The scores do not go beyond 160, and a scaled score of 19 does not reflect the ability of the child who passes far more than the minimal number of items needed to obtain that score. Overall the criticisms of WISC-R—inaccuracy at age extremes, difficulty in estimating the high-scoring child, and problems in assessing the poor and culturally different child—are the same as those for the Stanford Binet.

*Wechsler Preschool and Primary Scale of Intelligence (WIPPSI)* WIPPSI, another test designed by David Wechsler, is intended to be used with children from 3 years, 10 months, and 16 days to 6 years, 7 months, and 15 days.* It contains some questions taken from the original WISC plus new material. Its overall organization, in terms of IQ and scaled scores, is the same as that on WISC-R. The verbal tests are information, vocabulary, arithmetic, similarities, comprehension, and sentences (supplementary test). The performance tests are animal house, picture completion, mazes, geometric design, and block design. Like its big brother WISC-R, WIPPSI takes about one hour to administer. It tends to be infrequently used with gifted preschool children because many people feel its ceiling is too restrictive. The Stanford-Binet is more frequently the test of choice with the young gifted child.

*The McCarthy Scales of Children's Abilities*   This test, developed by Dorothea McCarthy in 1972, is another alternative to the Stanford-Binet. While its structure somewhat resembles WIPPSI, the age span it covers, 2½–8 years, is wider. Like the other individual tests, the McCarthy takes about an hour to administer. The scores provided are similar to IQ scores, but are not called IQs. The McCarthy has had somewhat more use with the educationally handicapped, rather than with the gifted. It has been used in the Seattle Gifted Project, but its effectiveness with gifted populations has yet to be determined.

### Quick Screening Tests

Quick screening tests are designed to allow a fairly accurate estimate in a short amount of time. While their results usually agree with more extensive tests, they frequently yield scores either somewhat higher or somewhat lower. The rea-

*The following material is from David Wechsler, *Manual for the Wechsler Preschool and Primary Scale of Intelligence* (New York: The Psychological Corporation, 1967). Copyright © 1963, 1967 by The Psychological Corporation. By permission of The Psychological Corporation.

son for this is that they tend to be focused on one or two specific skills, and not on the variety of skills the more extensive tests measure; these skills may just happen to be the child's strongest or weakest ability areas. Quick screens should not replace the use of an individual test, especially for individual planning. Some examples of this type of rapid screening test follow.

*Peabody Picture Vocabulary Test*   The Peabody is a nonverbal test of receptive vocabulary. It takes 10–15 minutes to give, and was designed for children 2½–18. The child is shown a series of pages, with each page containing four pictures, and asked to point to the correct picture, for example, "Show me the dog." Results are given in MA and IQ scores.

*Slosson Intelligence Test (SIT)*   Designed by Richard Slosson in 1963, this test takes about 20 minutes. It is a relatively multifactored screening measure used from infancy to adulthood. Items on the test are similar to those on the Binet. Test results give MA and IQ score.

*Raven Progressive Matrices*   The Raven test, developed by John Raven in 1956, takes somewhat longer to give than the two previous measures. It is designed for persons five and one-half years and up. It consists of a series of colored designs, suggestive of pattern fabric or wallpaper, with a section missing. The person must select from a series of samples the one that belongs in the hole in the main pattern. Results are given in percentiles.

### Abbreviated Test Forms

The vocabulary, information, similarities, and block-design portions of WISC-R are abbreviated individual tests that are frequently used as screening tools. While this method can identify many gifted children, it is not especially useful in planning. If we are to get away from rigid IQ cutoffs for gifted programs, and intend to individualize, then we must seek the most comprehensive assessment of skills possible.

# Creativity

### Creativity and Divergent Thinking

Once it was realized that intelligence had many factors, educators began to take a closer look at its components. Creativity is one area that traditional intelligence testing barely touches. If, as Guilford remarks, "intelligence is readiness to solve problems," present tests would not seem to allow creative persons the chance to demonstrate this facet of their abilities. Problem solving on traditional intelligence tests is largely a matter of convergent problem solving (finding the one best right answer).

There was a time when creativity was considered synonymous with divergent thinking, sometimes called "broad search." In divergent thinking, instead of focusing on the one best right answer to a problem, a person considers many alternatives. When you think divergently, you emphasize the number and variety of options.

Creativity in itself has many factors; divergent thinking is only one of them. Just as considering the tasks on IQ tests as the only measure of intelligence is too restrictive, so seeing crativity and divergency as one and the same is also too narrow.

## "The Small Cage Habit"

Creativity necessitates breaking old patterns of behavior, which is not an easy thing to do. It requires venturing into the unknown, with no concern that something may not work, or hasn't been done before. A good example of what we mean is illustrated in a story originally told by Bill Higginbotham, which was adapted by the *Journal of Creative Behavior* and published as "The Story of the Sad Bear." It is based on an incident that took place at the St. Louis Zoo, when animals were first removed from cages and placed in a "natural environment."

### The Story of the Sad Bear*

*Once upon a time there was a very sad bear who was kept in a very small cage in the town zoo. When the sad bear wasn't eating or sleeping, he occupied his time pacing . . . eight paces forward, and eight paces back again. Again and again he paced the parameters of his very small cage.*

*One day the zookeeper said, "It's sad to see this bear pacing back and forth in his confining cage. I shall build him a*

*"The Story of the Sad Bear," *The Journal of Creative Behavior*, 14, no. 2, (1980): i-iv. Published by The Creative Education Foundation, Inc. Reprinted by permission.

*great, open, and elegant space so that he may romp with
great freedom and abandon." And so he did.*

*As the space was completed, great waves of excitement
charged through the town, and finally, the magic day came
to move the bear to his new headquarters. The town Mayor
delivered an arousing invocation to the disdain of the
screaming hordes of harried children.*

*The municipal marching brass band manifested a brassy bra-
vado of sound that reached a crescendo at the glorious moment the sad bear was ushered into his elegant new quarters.
Whispers of curious expectation rose from the crowd as they
watched the great beast frozen in the uncertainty of the moment. Then the sad bear looked to his left, and to his right,
and then began to move . . . one step, two, five, eight paces
forward, and eight back again . . . again and again. To the
shocked amazement of the crowd, he paced the parameters of
his old very small cage.*

## Creativity Grows Up

Much of the systematic research on creativity began with J. P.
Guilford's theories and Paul Torrance's concepts in the early
1950s. The idea of divergent thinking made its appearance at
this time. Emphasis began to be placed on thinking that had
no predetermined answer. Those who defined creativity de-
manded that in a truly creative act concrete results must be
produced. Along the way "concrete product" was further defined as one that was "socially useful." In general, this is too
demanding a definition for creativity. We have mentioned
that the gifted child has the potential to produce socially useful acts; this holds true for creativity as well. Creativity in
children does not need to lead to a product that will immediately gain the child eminence. Creative thinking must be cultivated for its own sake; it needs help to survive during the
highly convergent (noncreative) school years. There is little
question that creative ability dips during stressful transition
times in school, for example at the beginning of elementary or
junior high school. Another such stress point is during the
fourth grade with the emergence of peer group pressures, a
time considered the most adverse for creative ability. Creative
ability may never be as great again after fourth grade as it was
before.

## Creativity and General Intellectual Ability

Above a score of 130, there is little relationship between the IQ score and creativity. However, researchers suggest that IQ scores may need to be at least as high as approximately 120 to, in Barbara Clark's words, "establish a base of knowledge broad enough to use the analytic . . . and evaluative thinking necessary for rational creative production." (Some researchers, such as Joseph Renzulli, suggest that the presence of above-average ability—such as a score of 110 or better—is sufficient for creative acts to take place.) Thus, while very superior ability is not a necessity in creative behavior, merely above-average skills may not be sufficient to produce the components of verbal or other types of creative acts. This view does not apply to children with a specific, isolated gift, as in art or music; here there may be little or no relationship between the talent and the child's other skills. Nevertheless, it often occurs that a child is gifted in more than one way. The child who appears to have only an isolated skill is generally the youngster who has not been identified as gifted.

Creativity, like other intellectual skills, is not like a disease you can "catch." When creative ability is exhibited unexpectedly in a child, you should not assume it is a skill that has just been acquired. It has always been part of the child's makeup but it was not evident before. We may not have a foolproof way of identifying every gifted person, nor does every gifted person always function as if he or she were gifted.

## Productive Problem Solving

Problem solving is a skill closely related to creativity. Some believe that because it involves novel responses to novel situations, problem solving has creative components. The main difference between problem solving and other creative acts is that problem solving is focused on the practical, recognized problem, while creative thinking in general frequently focuses on the impractical.

Problem solving suggests the need to use what Daniel Keating (82) calls "critical analysis." Critical analysis is the ability to make evaluative judgments about information or situations. The critical analysis involved in problem solving is the type of skill evidenced by the scientific method. It is interesting to note that very few children admitted into gifted and talented programs are skilled in problem solving. Most experts in gifted education indicate that evaluation is one type of intellectual skill that can and should be taught systematically.

## Other Aspects of Creativity

Besides the general category of divergent thinking, there are other types of creative behavior, some of which have been described by Frank Williams (103). One of these is fluency.

Fluency suggests the idea of quantity; it involves the number of relevant ideas presented by the individual. An example of fluency would be the responses to a question such as "List all the alternate sites for the town's power plant."

There has been some argument that we must be careful how we develop fluency. Some experts feel that a random reinforcement of fluency can be counterproductive. It may not be a good idea to list all the uses one can think of for a light bulb, a brick, or a toothpick. To be the most effective, fluency may need to be developed in the context of a relevant problem.

A second aspect of creativity described by Williams is original thinking. This is identical to the concept of uniqueness, and closely akin to divergence. It implies rareness or novelty. While there is no such thing as a totally original response, the creative or original thought occurs so rarely as to be considered unique. Originality is the ability to come up with the uncommon solution.

Another creativity skill is called flexible thinking in Williams's system or transformations in Guilford's system. This is the ability to make shifts in one's method of analysis. It is the opposite of the rigid approach to tasks. The flexible thinker can shift information from one category to another, from one approach to another, and is willing to accept and utilize new information on a subject when it suddenly appears on the scene.

Still another factor in creativity is elaborative thinking. This is the ability to add to what you or someone else has produced. It is the detail that fleshes out a concept. This is the type of thinking involved in making information clearly understood. Elaborative thinking is not vague. As with problem-solving skills, the elaborative-thinking skill is not generally among the strong points of many of the children entering gifted and talented programs, but it is a skill that can be shaped and increased. It deserves considerable attention in special programming.

To these skills Guilford would add implications, a highly abstract ability that goes beyond simple sequential logic. It suggests that the child is adept at deductive thinking. The child can hypothesize about an outcome yet to happen or about things that might have precipitated the situation. Implications skills are very much involved in productive problem solving.

Williams talks about the affective characteristics of creative thinkers. Such children are curious; they are risk takers, they are often described as very imaginative. Creatively gifted children like complexity and can tolerate chaos because they can bring order to the task themselves.

## The Creative Process

The creative process has been discussed thoroughly in the professional literature by a number of experts. James Gallagher, in *Teaching the Gifted Child* (33), has devised a system to divide and describe the four major stages in the creative process.

The first stage is one of preparation. It is a time of stating the problem precisely. It is characterized by curiosity about the problem and an intense focus of energy on it. According to Gallagher, it is one of the "neat and well organized" aspects of the creative process.

The second and third stages in creativity are most often thought of as divergent thinking. This is the time for trying out a variety of ideas. During these stages of the process, the work is often "sloppy" and seems "confused." The thinking process is marked by incubation and illumination. During incubation it may seem that the person is not actually working on the problem when in fact he or she really is very involved, even if this involvement is at a subconscious level. This is the time for risk taking, imagination, and a willingness to deal with mistakes and failure.

The final stage of the creative process is again very organized. Here the person must make judgments about the adequacy of the product and be prepared to alter it. This final stage Gallagher calls verification. In many ways this final stage is the most important because, if we do not learn to evaluate our own productions critically, we not only overlook errors but also miss chances for other interpretations of our findings.

## Creativity Tests

Many people have heralded creativity as the solution to the inaccuracy of intelligence measures in identifying gifted and talented students. Lest we expect too much from the assessment of creativity, let us look at some of the limitations on the evaluation of creativity as we know it today.

One of the facts that has been pointed to most strongly is that measures of creativity show a low relationship to IQ scores; this indicates that the two measures must be measuring different factors. Creativity tests may also be less biased against minority groups than intelligence tests and thus more "culturally fair" than general intelligence measures. However, there is as little relationship (or correlation) among the various creativity measures as there is between any of them and intellectual test results. This means that we are still not entirely sure exactly what type of creativity each test measures or how the different measures are related to creativity as a whole.

Another problem is that the mere presence of time limits on tests hinders the measuring of creative ability. In 1969 Barron (65) stated that creative individuals see creativity testing as too shallow and piecemeal, and find the time limits annoying.

Barbara Clark, in *Growing Up Gifted* (69), rightly states that part of the problem in measuring creativity is that it is difficult to assess the personality and emotional components of the process. Yet, even considering the limitations on interpreting creativity tests, they are a valuable aid in broadening our view of who the gifted person is.

There are other types of gifted abilities that are not tapped by either general intelligence or creativity tests. These are related to personality characteristics. We will address these skills in Chapter 4. For now, let us take a closer look at some of the creativity tests your child may encounter. Many of them still have their primary use in research on creativity rather than in evaluation of individuals. Because there is still so much debate about how independent each creativity skill is from all the others, test findings may tend to overlap. Successful use of these tests is obtained when they are employed in the context of an overall screening.

*Torrance Tests of Creative Thinking*   This test was designed by Paul Torrance in 1966, and has had one revision. It has five verbal subtests: Ask and Guess; Product Improvement; Unusual Uses; Unusual Questions; and Just Suppose. The nonverbal tasks are Picture Construction, Incomplete Figures, and Repeated Figures. It is a rather long test, taking several hours to administer. It is considered one of the major tests of creative thinking. Scoring and interpretation are difficult and require a trained professional with experience in testing. Results are given in such a way that they are not easily understood by lay persons.

*Creativity Tests for Children*   This test was designed by Guilford in 1971. It focuses on the divergent skills section of his Structure of Intellect model. Like most creativity tests, it is lengthy, having ten tasks for each of ten different abilities. Examples are: Names for Stories; Similar Meanings; and What To Do with It.

*Thinking Creatively with Sounds and Words*   This is actually two tests developed between 1965 and 1973. There are three authors involved: Cunnington, Torrance, and Khatena. The tests examine sound and word sets and require the person to let go of commonplace thinking.

*The Wallach and Kogan Creativity Battery*   Developed in 1965 for kindergarten through sixth grades, this is not a widely used test; it is favored for research.

## Summing Up

As with any new undertaking, you may not yet be as comfortable as you would like to be with the material we have presented. You may feel confused by what is being said and taught to you. Rest assured that as you become more familiar with the topic, these feelings will pass. What you are doing now is learning to view your gifted or talented child in a new way. Yes, you know this child better than anyone else does, but now you are being asked to look at him or her from a more technical perspective, as the educator is going to look at him or her. At some point you may feel that the "experts" are intruding on your life; at the same time you may be overjoyed that others see in your child something you've recognized all along.

This chapter has examined the nature of intelligence and creative behavior. The nature/nurture controversy is a long-standing one and probably will never be fully resolved to anyone's satisfaction. Educators and parents must attempt to help children fulfill as much of their potential as possible.

Intelligence has been shown to be multifactored, and any individual intelligence test is only as good as the person who administers, scores, and interprets it. If individual intelligence testing is to be done, the test should be administered by a certified or licensed psychologist. There have been too many "misinterpretations" by other educators, whose only use for an intelligence test is the IQ score. Intelligence testing is much more than that score; more sophisticated analysis is available when the evaluation is performed by an expert.

Creativity is also multifactored, but it is difficult to determine how the results of testing for creativity relate to the creative product itself. Since creativity seems to be as difficult to measure as intelligence, there are considerable differences of opinion as to its nature as well. Educators often feel they are treading on unsure ground when they discuss creativity testing.

While these measures of intelligence and creativity are the best we possess at the moment, we must always be willing to make improvements and progress. We must not remain content forever with the status quo or, like the story of the sad bear in the small cage, be reluctant to change.

# 4
# Demystifying Personality and Other Traits

B efore we discuss the characteristics of gifted children's personalities, we must give a general description of personality—with the understanding that there is no universally agreed on definition of personality by behavioral scientists. Most lay people look on personality as the way people present themselves during social interactions. Behavioral scientists insist on examining personality in a far more complex and concise manner. They define the abstract concept of personality as the unique group of traits that make up an individual. These traits, which are fairly consistent over time, distinguish one individual from another. Personality traits generally reveal themselves in a person's responses to various situations.

## How Personality Develops

An individual's personality does not spontaneously change over time. Change usually occurs only when there are critical circumstances that provoke it—a traumatic event, such as the death of a loved one, or therapeutic intervention. This is why it is difficult for people to alter their habits. Despite all the change taking place in the surrounding environment, individual personalities remain more or less constant. People need this consistency in order to know who they are and to feel secure in themselves. Think of yourself with a personality that shifts continually as the environment around you changes; you would find yourself confused, upset, and unable to make any decisions.

## Modeling

There are many theories that try to account for how our personalities develop. One theory is that we design our behavior on the example of others, a method called modeling. Research indicates that children learn from the important people around them, their parents being their most important models. Whether parents instruct directly or indirectly, consciously or unconsciously, they are still the prime teachers and personality makers of their children. This is true for any child, gifted or not, achiever or not. The parents and the home environment are the most important variables in what the child is and is likely to become.

## Identification

Prior to examining the child's interaction with others, we must discuss how a person develops the strong sense of self called identity. Children develop an identity or view of who they are from the world around them. The most important objects in their environment are generally adults, especially their parents. Important adults are those persons who reinforce the child's behavior. The child's first identification with the environment stems from his or her interaction with the mother or primary care giver. She is the important or reinforcing person fulfilling the child's needs. During the early stage of development, these needs are largely physiological and are fulfilled via nourishment, contact, and any other physical act that gives comfort. From this basic mother-child relationship, using the process of imitation, we begin to identify with or become like the important adults in our life.

The process of identification or imitation sets the stage for the child to learn to live in the everyday social world. Most of what children learn about how to deal with people and situations they acquire through imitation or identification. Young children are excellent imitators, to which any parent can at-test, especially when it is some unwanted behavior that is copied. We seem more likely to notice that our children are imitators when they do something we don't want them to do. Our toddler, for example, may have uttered more four-letter words than we care to remember.

The process of identification, according to many theorists, provides the core of what children are to become; it foreshad-ows the personality traits and social skills the child will ex-hibit later. Thus, the way we interact with our children and how we make them feel will be the way they interact with others. People must form their own identities before they can interact maturely with other people. This interaction is also called the socialization process.

## The Value of Self-Esteem

Children cannot form a positive identity unless they are given a way to develop positive self-esteem. Self-esteem is the man-ner in which people evaluate themselves and their interac-tions, and children learn to evaluate themselves in two major ways. First, they are encouraged directly by the important people in their lives. Encouragement begins with letting them know they are cared for, and that reliable people are doing the caring. Adults build reliability by behaving as consistently as possible while keeping the child's best interests in mind.

Encouragement should not be confused with a lack of dis-cipline. Children need discipline in order to learn about the normal boundaries of behavior. In addition, they view gentle discipline as a form of parental caring. Some parents are afraid to discipline their children for fear of harming them. On the contrary, problems arise in undisciplined children, who will seek out structure by constantly testing their parents' pa-tience. We have all suffered at one time or another when we were in the company of such children.

Likewise, it is not appropriate to eliminate all frustrations from children's lives. If they learn how to overcome small problems successfully, they will be equipped to handle larger frustrations later on as adults.

Giving children reinforcement and feelings of self-worth may seem elementary, but it can be difficult for some parents to do. It is important to be enthusiastic, to be sincere in your praise of your child's positive actions, and to offer encouragement continuously. Many parents find it much easier to discipline and focus on the child's negative behaviors. How often have you heard yourself saying "No" or "Stop" or "Don't do that"? How often do you say "That was a great effort" or "You've made a big improvement" or "I'm glad you are learning to make decisions"? If there are more negatives than positives, it may be time to take stock and change your behavior. Sometimes it helps to ask your spouse how many positive things you say to your children; it is generally easier to look at someone else's behavior than it is to monitor one's own actions.

Besides directly supporting feelings of self-esteem, parents can communicate such feelings if they themselves have positive self-regard. Children identify with parental feelings as well as behavior, and that includes feelings of self-esteem. If you feel like a worthwhile person, your children in turn will feel that way about themselves. Many parents of gifted children are trying to relive their own lives through their children; they push the children to do the things they wish they had done for themselves. This type of behavior frequently alienates the child. Take the case of a boy whose mother had been living her life through him. The boy refused to work in school. When the mother returned to college and began a career, she learned to value a wider variety of her skills, and lost the need to demand perfection in all that her son tried; as a result his school work improved notably.

# The Myth of the "Gifted Personality"

Many parents and some educators seem to believe that gifted and talented children possess a single personality type that is unique and sets them apart from the balance of the population. This is not true. Gifted children have as diverse personalities as any other group of youngsters. Much of what parents and teachers are seeing when they talk about a unique personality is actually a temperament style. For example, many teachers are more likely to identify children for a gifted and talented program if the youngsters are what is termed "easy" children.

Easy children are a teacher's dream. They are predictable, generally pleasant, and willing to do things any way the teacher likes. Don was one such child. He was nominated twice for a gifted and talented program. His achievement scores were good, and his group IQ test score was above average. However, analysis of his individual IQ test on two separate testings did not reveal any special strengths; his overall functioning level on both intelligence measures was consistently average. This raised questions about the actual existence of his gifts. Don was neither culturally deprived nor handicapped in any way. Although he had been part of an "enriched" classroom for several years, his teachers reported that he was not especially creative, nor did he display special talent in art, music, or leadership. They thought Don was academically gifted simply because he was polite, cheerful, worked hard, and rarely presented a behavior problem. Obviously Don was a well-adjusted, able student who could be looked to with pride by both his parents and teachers. It was very doubtful, however, that he was academically gifted.

At the opposite extreme is the "difficult" child, who often appears oppositional, negative, and stubborn. Difficult children are given to wide swings of mood, being happy and cooperative one minute and sullen and resistive the next. As preschoolers, they will not let their parents show them how to do anything, from getting dressed to riding a tricycle. As students, they cannot tolerate any explanation of a problem or method of analysis that varies markedly from their own. Sometimes difficult children have trouble "reading" (understanding) their environment, which only encourages them to be even more rigid in their beliefs.

George is typical of the difficult child. When he was almost eleven, his teacher felt that he was fairly good as a student, but he rarely remained in his seat or paid attention to directions. George spent much of his time wandering about, making paper airplanes, and annoying other children. He was not well accepted by his peers because he tended to point out their shortcomings, loudly. He was equally disliked by his teacher because of his contrary nature. However, George seemed able simply to "pick up" information from the verbal interactions in the classroom, and he used the information well on tests. Evaluation revealed a boy with a remarkable memory pattern as well as many other strong areas. While George's overall performance was "only" in the lower end of the superior range, it was apparent that his contrary tendencies had extended into the testing session and had probably kept him from scoring as well as he might have under better conditions. George's teacher recognized that he was bright, but because of his behavior she had not thought to identify him as gifted.

A third type of temperament might be best described as "wary" or, as Wendy Roedell and her coauthors describe it in *Gifted Young Children* (54), "slow-to-warm up." Victor is a good example of this third pattern. He was a very quiet, even somewhat hostile boy, especially when first confronting unfamiliar adults. He seemed to measure every word he said and watch every move the adults made; he questioned directions at almost every opportunity. Victor tried to present himself initially as a difficult child, but after he had settled into a situation, he dropped his sullen facade and his behavior changed. He was then very open and quite verbal, and displayed keen insight into personal interactions. Victor is, in actuality, the alert, pleasant youngster this second view suggested. However, at the beginning of each school year, or at any time Victor must adjust to new people or changes in routine or environment, he reverts to his wary behavior. It is a good defense for his own anxiety, but it does not aid in an accurate assessment of his academic needs. Wary children are frequently overlooked in screening either because the teacher reacts to their initial withdrawal or hostility, or because the staff is given the mistaken notion that the child is too shy and immature to benefit from a special program.

## Behavior Traits: Predictors or Illusions?

Psychologists often believe that past behavior is a predictor of future behavior. But predicting giftedness in children is often an illusion. One set of characteristics will not *always* foreshadow the way a person will act in the future. We can never be certain that one set of traits always has a one-to-one relationship with some other behavior.

Parents are frequently bombarded with lists of characteristics describing what gifted children are supposed to be like. As we have seen, there are in reality profound individual differences among the gifted and talented, and we should be very cautious about making generalizations. Rather than reproduce a list of traits, let us discuss some specific characteristics that gifted children have been seen to display.

## Sensitivity

Gifted children have been described as being very sensitive and very aware individuals. This doesn't mean that all gifted children have "cornered the market" on perceptiveness. What it does mean is that high levels of sensitivity and awareness are common among gifted children. While the mere presence of sensitivity does not identify a child as gifted, it should signal us to examine the case further. Janet and Marion are two good examples of perceptive gifted children.

During individual testing, Janet was expertly solving a series of "pattern problems." She found the exercise particularly simple and made numerous remarks about the task as she completed each card. At one point, she stopped before the next example, and commented that what really made the test harder at that point was that the guide lines of the pattern had been removed. This certainly was not a common observaton, and it suggested that Janet was aware of far more aspects of the task than what had been given in the directions.

While Janet demonstrates alertness in a learning situation, Marion exhibits exceptional social awareness. Marion and Randy were in the same gifted and talented class. Randy was always the butt of the older boys' jokes and had difficulty in standing up for his rights. The staff was concerned and made several attempts to intervene, but to no avail. Marion, on the other hand, was very popular with the other children, and was often looked to for leadership. One day things had gone especially badly for Randy, and he was standing on the sidelines. Marion remarked to her teacher that if Randy just stood up once to the older boys they would leave him alone. The teacher asked Marion how she felt Randy might learn to do this. Marion thought a minute, and asked if they couldn't simulate a few encounters to help Randy get some ideas. The teacher was impressed that Marion drew a connection between the social studies simulations the class had been doing and this situation. Such social perceptiveness was a typical characteristic of Marion's behavior. It was evidenced at home as well as in school.

Victor, whom we described earlier, also is a socially aware child. At age eight, when describing a conflict he was having with his mother, he remarked, "She never answers your questions directly. She's always evasive. It makes me very angry when I feel like she's not telling the truth."

Gifted children also see more of a complete picture when viewing an interaction, and their reactions will often reflect this degree of sophistication. But good social awareness does not always produce the ability to socialize well. Sally exemplifies this inconsistency.

Sally had poor relationships with her peers. She tended to be bossy and opinionated and had a very quick temper. By turns, the other children either shunned her or tried to provoke an outburst. Sally was acutely aware of her unpopularity. At one point she went so far as to write to an advice column in her local newspaper. But as aware as she was, she could no more deal with it on her own than could any nongifted child. Sally's intelligence had no relationship to her ability to cope socially.

Sensitivity has its negative aspects as well. The insecure individual may understand something at an intellectual level, but the comprehension will not diminish his or her anxiety level. The child's anxiety may in fact increase depending on the circumstances surrounding his or her actions.

## Idealism

Gifted children frequently are idealistic, but often they don't know how to convince others of their ideas. The result may be that they serve their cause but alienate their friends. Karen serves a good example.

Karen attended an old-fashioned elementary school where the grades went from first to eighth. It was a tradition at the school to give the children in the last two or three grades jobs such as hall monitor. Great stress was placed on the responsibility of these jobs and on the need for monitors to treat all classmates alike, whether friends or not. This sense of values created a great impression on Karen. When it was her turn to serve, she was determined to do a "perfect" job. Unfortunately, Karen's idealism got the better of her. She became a tyrant, and made everyone live by the letter of the school rule book. At times her interpretation of the rules was more stringent than the staff's. Not only did Karen not favor her friends, she tended to be even more exacting with them than with the other children. Needless to say, by the end of the year Karen had very few friends left. The other children so disliked her that her teachers decided to take away her authority. Karen was shocked. She could not comprehend why the children resented her and the staff no longer desired her to continue the job. It was many years before she realized what had happened to her during that year of school.

Not all gifted children are gifted communicators. Idealists need to temper how they present views to a disinterested audience, and not try to cram things down their throats. One of the roles of an effective program for the gifted should be not only to train for sensitivity and idealism, but to help children use these skills productively.

## Intensity

Another characteristic of personality that has both good and bad aspects to it is intensity of feeling. Teachers of the gifted will be the first to attest that these children are frequently passionate in their views. Sometimes this commitment amounts to stubbornness. it is important to help gifted children differentiate between fact and emotion, so that they are not totally controlled by their own emotions. This single-mindedness can help them lose sight of the real issues in a situation or the ability to react flexibly.

The Renzulli-Hartman checklist in Chapter 5 ("Scale for Rating Behavioral Characteristics of Superior Students") provides further illustrations of what are often considered common characteristics of the gifted and talented. As with the developmental checklists examined in an earlier chapter, parents should use care in interpreting the scale. Not all children will display all the characteristics it lists. It is meant to serve as a means of helping staff and parents focus on behavior that many times indicates exceptional potential.

## Overall Adjustment

Studies have indicated that the gifted population is often better able to adjust to their environment than other groups. Other data also indicate better social awareness and more personal security among the gifted. However, the more extremely gifted children seem to have comparatively greater difficulties than others. A possible explanation for this may lie in their more sophisticated intellectual assessment of situations. One boy could not understand why his fifth-grade classmates were so illogical. Why would they bother to make fun of each other, or try to outdo each other? Wouldn't it be more appropriate, he explained, if we all tried to be helpful to each other and avoided silly conflicts? This extremely gifted child could not understand that it was perfectly natural for fifth graders to be competitive, even when it was to the detriment of others. Consequently, he alienated his peers by his judgmental attitude.

Gifted children may also experience frustration when their intellectual development outstrips their physical maturity. For example, a five-year-old who can read and reason like a ten-year-old may not have the visual motor coordination necessary to write out his thoughts. Many youngsters would be extremely frustrated by such a gap.

## Genius or Insanity

When people talk about the extremely gifted, they frequently express the notion that genius borders on insanity. This is definitely not true. Mental illness can be manifested at any level of intelligence. It is possible that the notion is fostered by the prominence of certain gifted individuals who have had psychiatric problems. Kathleen Montour suggests the example of William James Sidis, whose personal tragedy is often associated with the myth. Sidis went from early eminence to oblivion, starting with a brilliant school career and ending up in a menial job, the sorry product of his father's obsession to produce the "ideal man." However, it was his father's ceaseless pushing and parading of William's accomplishments—not his intelligence—that was the cause of his failure. In her article "William James Sidis" (22), Montour states that even as a young baby Sidis was beginning to exhibit a maladjusted personality. By the time he received his B.A. from Harvard at age 16, his emotional difficulties were fully in bloom. "He would distract a class whenever he was bored and had been rude to his questioners when he gave his famous lecture [on Four Dimensional Bodies]. . . . But, as he grew older, interviews showed him to be quite warped in his outlook. He refused ever to consider marrying, and thought being totally cut off from people was the perfect life."

The fact is that a person with average intelligence will not generally rise to a position of sufficient prominence to attract public attention to any psychological problems he may have. In the same way, the individual, gifted or not, who exhibits a well-adjusted personality rarely receives special notice. Much negative attention was paid to the academic acceleration that many educators credited with Sidis's problems. On the other hand, Montour points to Norbert Weiner, the father of cybernetics, who graduated from Tufts at age 14 and who had a highly successful personal and professional life. The evidence suggests that gifted and talented individuals need careful and balanced guidance. It is not their intelligence itself that will lead them into difficulties, but their interactions with the significant people in their lives.

# Underachievers

There have been numerous studies of the gifted underachiever. Underachievement in its most simple terms is the condition of not working up to one's potential. Professionals in the field often debate about an exact definition so that underachievement can be researched properly; a more detailed description would also help parents to avoid "misdiagnosing" their children as underachievers.

## Who They Are

Identifying an underachiever in the schools is not especially difficult once you know some basic information about the child. This information usually includes some idea of the child's potential, such as IQ level and present functional achievement level. For example, if we are dealing with a child of average ability, we would expect that child to be, within certain limits, performing on grade level academically. An academically gifted child of superior to very superior ability would be expected to be achieving at least two to three years above grade level. This does not mean that every subject or academic skill should be at or above this level. There are exceptions to every rule, and as we have previously noted, each child, even if academically gifted, will have relative strengths and weaknesses. If you are not sure about your youngster's performance but suspect a discrepancy between achievement and potential, it is best to seek some advice from school personnel.

Besides the basic rule of thumb we have just provided, underachievers display a variety of other characteristics. They may appear to dislike school or try to get by with just the minimum of work. Their peer group may consist of children who likewise are not interested in school. Even involved, concerned parents may harbor an underachiever in the house. Underachievement is a complex phenomenon and is produced by many factors. Before we discuss the general approaches for dealing with it, let us take a closer look at the problem itself. Underachievement is not just a lower-class or minority problem. It cuts across all social groups, although its origins may vary depending on the section of the population.

## Becoming an Underachiever

Probably one of the most frustrating children for the teacher or psychotherapist to work with is the gifted underachiever. Here is a person of tremendous potential who rarely or never uses this ability because of overwhelming internal influences, which often have their early beginnings in the family. James Gallagher, in *Teaching the Gifted Child* (33), gives a thorough summary of the dynamics behind the underachieving personality. Gallagher, like many other specialists in gifted education, feels that the problem is intensified by a rigid system that cannot shift its policies to meet the needs of these children.

Gifted underachievers initially will mask their high ability very well. Thus, most people do not perceive that they are dealing with a gifted individual. Many times, however, the teacher does realize that the child has above-average ability, and makes a referral for psychological evaluation. Individual testing may then reveal the high potential of the child. While underachievers can behave in many different ways, the overriding personality dynamics appear to be passivity and a poor self-concept (which we have earlier referred to as self-esteem).

Every once in a while there may be a "spark" from the underachiever. There may be an unexpected response to a question, a good paper, an ingenious suggestion, or some similar behavior that appears out of character with the child's usual level of achievement. The astute teacher will pick this discrepancy up and investigate the situation further. Such erratic behavior can be easily attributed to chance, however, and is overlooked by many teachers.

One gifted, underachieving boy, Peter, spent most of his school years with such a passive approach to school. What was most striking about his behavior was a tendency always to do well enough academically to move up to the next educational level. Thus he went from just getting by in high school to just making it in college, to just graduating from college and getting into a graduate program eventually leading to a doctorate. He related that he often received great pleasure when he accomplished something or outdid someone when no one expected him to succeed. Unfortunately for this young man, as well as others like him, underachievement does not end with mediocre school performance. It can taint a person's adult accomplishments as well as his social interactions outside the classroom. The case of Emily also reflects the underachieving personality pattern

## A Case Study

Emily was the oldest girl in a large family. As a young child, she was brash, outspoken, and somewhat aggressive. Though she was obviously very alert, she chose a middle of the road, average academic stance in elementary school. She rarely failed or did poorly at anything, but then she was never outstanding either. Only one skill stood out, and that was spelling. Emily could spell anything. It almost seemed as if she spent hours reading the dictionary. However, her teachers shrugged off this ability as unimportant, and Emily continued along her unremarkable academic career. Junior and senior high revealed more of the same pattern. Emily stayed comfortably in the background, and was not included in the honors program. Right after high school, she left home and moved to another part of the country, where she applied for a job with a large company. In the process of their personnel screening, the staff discovered that Emily possessed very high ability indeed; her scores would have qualified her for a gifted and talented program at school. Because her high school courses had been so watered down, the company offered to train Emily for a rather sophisticated technical position. This offered Emily the chance to enter a field where she could have made rapid advancement and even won national attention. But rather than being overjoyed at the opportunity, Emily refused the training. Instead she took a more or less ordinary position with the company, well below her abilities. Emily stayed with the company for a couple of years and then drifted off to a similar position with another firm. Today she complains about her economic prospects but is still unwilling to better her education or to train for a more appropriate job. The underachiever pattern that Emily began to follow in elementary school has tagged along with her all her life. While she is clearly a person of great potential, Emily has never come close to working up to her ability. She longs for the better things in life, but seems unable to make a commitment to go out and earn them for herself.

Emily's pattern is typical of many gifted underachievers. They may pretend that they can do anything they want; but if they don't produce over a long enough period of time, the ability to accomplish things withers.

## Family Entanglements

We have in our society many gifted adults who are not producing for themselves or for society what they are capable of producing. Most gifted underachievers, whether child or adult, attribute their misfortunes and ill luck in life not to themselves but to forces outside their control. Although they are gifted, these individuals are too close to the problem to understand that their attitudes and self-defeating behaviors come from within themselves, and from their families.

Certain families breed underachievement in their children. For instance, there are parents who do not regard education very highly or who see it only as a means to earn more money. They fail to reinforce school performance, and are generally indifferent to their child's academic accomplishments. Other parents, with low self-esteem, do not believe their children can achieve academic success, and they communicate to their children such attitudes as low tolerance for frustration, passivity, a lack of self-respect, and a lack of high goals. As a result, the child learns an immature way of dealing with the world.

Some families give very little love or affection to their children. Although such parents can readily express anger and hostility, they cannot get close to their children. When the mother does express affection, she may do so inconsistently— she may act indifferent to the child's accomplishments at one time, but display concern and high anxiety when the child is in danger of failing. Such behavior is called giving "mixed signals." The child reacts to such unpredictability with confusion, anger, and disruptive behavior.

This is not meant to suggest that such parents do not love their children. They simply do not realize that their attitudes and behavior are reinforcing poor academic achievement.

Such parents may have little control over their behavior; they may simply be acting in the way they themselves were raised. Underachievement is a vicious cycle that can continue from one generation to another.

Underachieving children may demonstrate antischool and antisocial behavior. Because they may not have had positive experiences with significant authority figures, they may also be antagonistic to authority. This attitude may not be demonstrated by overt aggression, but is more likely to appear in passive-aggressive behavior. Such children do not actively disobey the wishes of adults, but they offer only minimal cooperation. Underachieving children have low self-esteem and much of their behavior is based on the need to protect their self-image. Thus, they often act defensive and distrustful, avoiding commitment ot anyone or anything. They will do anything in order to save face. The underachiever's unconscious reasoning can go something like this: If I try and fail (which underachievers assume is inevitable), I'll feel awful. I will not feel that I am a worthwhile person. If I don't try, and then fail, it won't matter because I can always say I didn't try, and I didn't care anyway.

Studies have shown that most male underachievers have had a negative relationship with their fathers. Their fathers have been distant or too involved with their own concerns to worry about their sons' progress. Peter, related that he often looked to other adult males for his close relationships. At different times in his life he copied the characteristics of different men, beginning with a favorite uncle, and progressing to a teacher, a boss, and a colleague; eventually he learned how to behave and in limited ways took on their values. Unfortunately, most of the relationships of male underachievers are either short-lived or superficial. Because they have not learned to be close to their fathers, they have difficulty getting close to others.

While the fathers of male underachievers tend to be hostile and rejecting of their sons, the mothers may be high in the controlling behavior that psychologists call authoritarianism. This type of woman is usually very conforming herself, and her feelings and thinking reflect a high level of control (of herself and others). Extreme conformity and control will certainly prod the divergent (nonconforming) personality toward rebellion. The son of this type of mother will generalize his feelings about her to the demanding, controlling, convergent teacher in his school. Such transference of feeling begins early in the school career of male underachievers.

In contrast, the mothers of underachieving girls tend to be low in authoritarianism. Such girls begin to exhibit poor academic performance later in their school careers than do underachieving boys—usually in the early high school years, while boys who underachieve tend to have been poor performers since the early elementary grades.

It is noteworthy that most of the studies on underachievement in gifted children focus on boys. Are there fewer gifted girls who underachieve? Or do parents and educators expect less from girls, so that their lowered performance is not viewed as underachievement?

A summary of research on underachievers' families suggests that they are much different from the families of achievers. The achiever's family often has parents with a higher educational level, more involved fathers, less controlling mothers, and more opportunity and encouragement of individual development. The families of underachievers tend to have parents with a lower educational level, children who are not anxious to please their parents, a distant relationship in general between parent and child, and at best a neutral and indifferent attitude toward education and success in general. Interviews with underachievers indicate that they tend to "hang out" with their peers, with whom they seem to feel more comfortable. These peers are similar to each other in their attitudes and their families are also fairly alike. This is certainly not an unexpected finding.

Peter related that while he was in high school he had two sets of friends. One set consisted of achievers with whom he could get together in school. If he saw any of these boys after school hours, he avoided all reference to his parents, and would never encourage these boys to come to his home. He was enthralled with their families, however, and many times seemed to form an attachment to the fathers of these friends. While he liked their life-style and at times contemplated being like them, this boy was really much more comfortable with his underachieving peers. He felt he had more in common with this second group, and was not merely a spectator in the progress of their lives. He tried not to discuss his achieving friends with them, however, because he feared their reaction.

Can we turn the situation around for underachievers? Because the problem lies largely within the family structure, the chances of altering the children's lives is slim unless the family is willing to change. Early identification and encouragement by the school system may be one key. The parents of underachievers must become involved in the educational process if there are to be lasting effects. For the gifted, as for the handicapped, the role of family support is vital. School systems trying to enlist such support should endeavor to develop parents' groups. Within that context it may be possible to educate those who can turn around the academic achievement of gifted underachievers.

# The Myth of the Overachiever

With almost the same breath that one child is called an underachiever, another is labeled an overachiever. What are overachievers? They are creatures similar to unicorns—many people talk as if they were real when in fact they don't exist. Whom do teachers label overachievers? Any child who seems to be producing more academically than what the teacher would expect, based on the all-powerful group IQ score. Let us examine the situation more carefully. Intelligence, if we could measure it totally, is like a full glass of water. Once it is full you can't add anything to it. The glass cannot be overfilled. If a child produces more than you would expect from the IQ score, there is something wrong with the score; the test is probably underestimating the child's ability. This will not be surprising when you remember that group intelligence tests assess very few intellecutal skills.

Another circumstance may be involved in the label "overachiever": The teacher may not be realistic in judging the difficulty of the assignments. The teacher may believe the assignment to be difficult, but it may be well within the child's abilities when the child works in a consistent and diligent manner. The result is that the child's productivity looks better than in reality it is. Inaccuracy in judging a child's ability is not an uncommon occurrence. The able learner who acts in a conforming manner is a lot more likely to impress the teacher than is the gifted child who can't be bothered with board work or filling in all the math examples in a workbook.

Overachievement is an illusion. What looks like over-achievement is really a matter of inaccurate tests, misjudgments about the difficulty of tasks facing the child, or misconceptions about performance based on the child's conforming behavior. If your son or daughter seems to be achieving higher than the group IQ test score suggests, forget the score and focus on the achievement.

## Stereotypes

Ever hear it said that gifted children spend all their time reading? Somehow the person on the street has envisioned the gifted child as a small, frail individual with horn-rimmed glasses, who never goes out in the open air or, if he or she does, is totally lacking in athletic ability. As Seagoe (56) explains, Lewis Terman demonstrated in 1925 that gifted children actually possessed superior physical characteristics; however, his study was based on middle- or upper-class children who came from advantaged environments, with the best medical care and nutrition. More recent research has discovered little or no relationship between physical characteristics and high intellectual ability. Just as gifted children vary greatly in terms of their intellectual profiles, so they vary in terms of physical traits and athletic skills. However, high intellectual ability and physical talent can and often do go together. For example, Bill Bradley, a New Jersey state senator, was a Rhodes scholar as well as a professional basketball star prior to his political career. Gifted children may excel at only one skill or at many different skills.

Let's take Glen for an example. In the first chapter we examined his development compared to that of his siblings, David and Marion. Glen is an exceptionally gifted youth who breaks nearly all the old stereotypes about gifted children. At 15 he is tall, handsome, well spoken, an adolescent with an easy manner when relating to either peers or adults. Glen deals with stress well. He once took an individual test as part of a class demonstration, and handled the situation with such aplomb that he could joke with the audience while performing at a very superior level.

Academically Glen is one of the top two or three students in his honors track. He consistently receives grades in the 90s, and has received 100 on a state exam. His academic interests span a wide variety of topics from Chinese culture to science. But while Glen does put effort into his classwork, his mother often complains that Glen is getting his top grades without extending himself in the least.

At the same time that he excels academically, Glen does well in sports and has participated on many teams. His friends look to him for leadership and he often serves as "judge" in their disputes. While they tease him about his facility in both academics and sports, Glen's friends don't seem to resent him. While he is not the only type of gifted child, he does dispel the stereotyped image—clear evidence that the gifted child does not have to be a friendless loner closeted with books. Educators must avoid setting up stereotypes of gifted and talented youngsters if they are to start a realistic approach to identifying them.

## Summing Up

Personality formation is a complex matter that involves contributions from the significant persons in a child's life. This is not to say that physical aspects don't have their place in personality development. Children with extreme emotional or cognitive difficulties often have physical concomitants (such as genetic or chemical aberrations, neurological impairment, etc.). However, in regard to gifted and talented individuals who fall within the normal range of personality development, it is probable that physical factors contribute less to the development of personality than do environmental ones.

Underachievement in gifted individuals is probably one of the most important problems in education of the gifted. In one sense, the movement to gifted and talented education is addressing itself to the issue of underachievement—both in working with the individual gifted underachiever and in trying to make sure that we get the most out of those gifted and talented individuals who are already trying to achieve. The gifted movement is trying to ensure that gifted children are given every opportunity to develop to their potential and not drift into underachievement because of educational circumstances beyond their control.

We shall make one last observation about the importance of the family in the development of a person's life. Although the nuclear family has been until now the most important factor in an individual's development, this situation may not continue unchanged. Institutions outside the home are increasingly taking over roles that used to be the province of the family. This trend has been evolving for quite some time, but it may be a double-edged sword. Schools, day-care centers, and other community groups may do many things better than does the nuclear family, such as sharing significant ideas and spreading the importance of getting along with others. But the home is better constituted to ensure individuality. It can encourage personality differences that will stimulate creative behavior and guarantee variety in society. Ideally, society will reach a balance where our children can have the best of both worlds.

A word of caution is in order regarding how much we can demand from institutions such as the schools. The schools should and must have programs to ensure equal education for the gifted and talented. Yet they cannot be expected to do everything. Families in the community must demand from themselves many of the things they would like to see developed in their children. This requires that parents take an active part in their children's upbringing. It may also require them to work harder to develop in themselves the positive skills and traits they would like their children eventually to develop.

# 5
# *Loss of Innocence: The Elementary School Years*

*The gifted were once almost completely neglected. Now everybody is hugging them to death.*
BRUMBAUGH AND ROSHCO

O ne philosophy of education holds that educational opportunity should be offered equally to everybody; another holds that each child should receive according to need, as opposed to the same education for all. In education, we have only begun to realize that the concept "the greatest good for the greatest number" has been overemphasized. Equal education means appropriate education and appropriate education means special, well-developed programs for the gifted and talented. When administrators are designing programs for the gifted and talented, they need to plan for a consistent, long-range commitment, not just a short-term scramble for scarce natural resources in times of crisis. The program descriptions in this chapter mostly reflect what can be done at the elementary school level.

Besides the children, a gifted and talented program has three major components: the teacher, the curriculum, and the organization or grouping of the students. While it is not necessarily the most important variable, the organization of the program is frequently the facet that educators focus their attention on. Because school systems have placed so much emphasis on ability groupings, we will discuss this factor first. Bear in mind that ability grouping in itself is not considered a sufficient provision for the gifted and talented, either by experts in the field or by many states that have come forth with policies on gifted education. (State policies vary considerably and are too voluminous to be discussed here. An excellent summary of them is available in *Creating Programs for the Gifted* (70) by Corinne P. Clendening and Ruth Ann Davies.)

## Types of Ability Groupings

Ability grouping has been called "provisions that facilitate the student's access to special learning opportunities." Several types of grouping are possible.

### Homogeneous Grouping

Homogeneous grouping is what many adults may remember as a tracking system. Here, all the students in a class are of similar intellectual ability and are functioning at fairly similar academic achievement levels. Homogeneous grouping can be as narrowly defined as a child's participation in an honors class for a specific subject at the secondary level, or it can be an old-fashioned tracking system at the elementary level or even a totally separate special school.

At the elementary school level, homogeneous grouping is appropriate only for the most highly (or "severely") gifted children. Children of only moderate gifted ability may in fact suffer more from this type of placement than they may gain. Full-time homogeneous grouping is generally inappropriate for culturally different and handicapped gifted students, because they are not always ready to compete in a total program with their nonhandicapped peers. Being isolated from the rest of the school population or being uprooted from the home school to attend a full-time magnet school is just as stressful for the gifted as it is for the handicapped in full-time special education placement. Full-time homogeneous grouping is beneficial for highly gifted children whose learning needs are so different that they require separate programming in nearly all subject areas. It is inappropriate for children who have a specific area of high academic potential, such as math, or who are talented in nonacademic areas, such as art. After all, giftedness is a wide category, taking in children of unusual potential from categories as diverse as leadership and general intellectual ability.

Homogeneous grouping is at its most useful when it is employed part-time for specific subject areas and full-time for the child highly gifted in general intellectual ability.

## Clustering

Clustering involves putting several children (usually from 3 to 8) in an otherwise fairly heterogeneous classroom. It is somewhat more effective when the ability spread in the classroom is not too broad. Planning and giving individualized attention to the cluster are easier if the balance of the class is of average or better ability. The elimination from the class of as many learning and behavior problems as possible is also desirable, so that the teacher is not overwhelmed by the variety of needs he or she must cater to. Socially, clustering allows the children to associate with others who may have similar interests and abilities. It is suited to the needs of all but the most highly gifted. It tends not to penalize those children with specific talents, or those who are gifted but also handicapped in some manner. Done properly, clustering encourages individual planning and can keep gifted children from becoming isolated.

## Pullout Programs

There are two types of pullout programs, centralized and decentralized. In a centralized pullout program—also called a magnet-school concept—gifted or talented children from around a school district are bused to one facility in the district. The amount of time spent at the magnet school may vary from a few hours to several days each week. Spending one full day at a magnet school is a typical arrangement. The problems with the concept are that the majority of the child's time may be spent inappropriately, that teachers generally demand that all missed work be made up, and that activities at the gifted and talented program itself are often too fragmented to be useful. There are also the administrative difficulties of transportation foul-ups, attendance, and resentment by teachers at the home school. Administrative advantages are the program's relatively low cost for staffing and supplies.

The second type of pullout program is decentralized, and

often takes place at a resource center set up within the home school. The children go for varied amounts of time to a resource room in their home school—such as a library or media center—and work with a special teacher. In all but the smallest districts, this is probably an itinerant teacher who is assigned to two or more schools. Ideally, a teacher should be assigned to each building, but this is a costly setup and therefore not practical where money is limited.

The advantages of an in-house pullout program are that it allows children to keep in contact with their regular class on pullout days, and it reduces teacher alienation, allows students to keep track of their work in the regular class, and avoids transportation difficulties. It also allows the itinerant teacher to work with the home class teacher in developing curriculum. In-house pullouts may also be less fragmented than a magnet-school approach. The major disadvantage of the program is that much of the work may still not be appropriate, although this may be less the case than in the magnet school because of the interaction with the regular teacher. Another major problem is that access to materials, especially "hardware," such as computers, or cameras, is rather restricted. Usually the only materials available are those owned by the individual school, or those the itinerant teacher can carry from place to place. Another minor disadvantage is that the students do not come in contact with children from the rest of the district as they would in the magnet school. Some educators believe that the magnet setting is more likely to relieve feelings of isolation among gifted and talented children by providing interaction with a larger and more varied number of their peers.

## Special Summer, Weekend, or After-School Programs

This type of program resembles a club, especially when it takes place after school or on weekends. In many ways, the structure is similar to other pull-out groupings. While such a program can offer some enrichment or specialized courses, it is even more fragmented than other types of pullout classes. The after-school class tends to be viewed as unrelated to the regular school program. The advantage to this is that it eliminates teacher resentment. The disadvantage may be in obtaining and retaining qualified staff. Gifted children themselves may be less than willing to participate in these programs, because they often have already filled their spare time with their own pursuits and interests. Such programs are best utilized when they are offered by an institution other than the school system, such as a local university or parent group, which makes them more attractive to students and parents because they are seen as an offering in addition to what the district itself supplies instead of a shoddy replacement for a better-developed model.

### The Ideal Model

Probably the best setting for the mildy and moderately gifted would be classroom clustering with an in-house pullout program. Access should be available to a centralized resource center where reference materials and hardward are kept. The advantage of this combination grouping is that it does not force children with dissimilar strengths and weaknesses to compete with each other, and encourages continuity and co-operation between the resource teacher and the regular teacher. The combination program is the closest we can come to total planning without homogeneous grouping. Those children who are so highly gifted that most of the school day is inappropriate for them will probably be best served in special schools; the disadvantage there of social isolation will be balanced by the flexible scope and pace in their overall program or special talent areas.

# Acceleration

An issue closely tied to grouping is acceleration. Many parents and educators react with extreme disfavor to the mere mention of the term. This is probably because acceleration has been overused and misused in the past. In actual fact, acceleration can yield positive results when properly employed. According to Clendening and Davies (70) acceleration consists of "activities that promote learning beyond [the] regularly prescribed curriculum." Barbara Clark, in *Growing Up Gifted* (69), cites some dozen studies showing that acceleration can provide positive results. Socially, it allows mature gifted students to associate with older children (whom they frequently would have picked as friends anyway). Despite the mistaken conception that it leads to social maladjustment, studies have indicated that in an accelerated program the well-adjusted gifted child tends to remain socially well adjusted. Acceleration reduces boredom and allows earlier entrance into careers that frequently have protracted training periods. In certain fields, such early entrance may be vital to future productivity. Some mathematicians speculate that the best-quality work in their field is often accomplished prior to 30 years of age, an age at which many people are barely out of graduate school.

Acceleration is not appropriate for all gifted students. It is best suited to those who evidence a high general level of academic superiority or who would benefit through acceleration in a specific skill such as music or math. Acceleration can take a variety of different forms, each of which must be considered with the individual child in mind. Let us discuss some of these different options.

### Early Admissions to Kindergarten

Many school districts set an age requirement for kindergarten entrance. Usually this restriction states that "the child must be five years old on or before December 1 (or December 31) of the kindergarten year." It is quite true that a large number of children who fulfill this age requirement are not ready for kindergarten. However, it is equally true that many gifted children born within a couple of months of this artificial cutoff are more ready for formal schooling than their slightly older peers. Considerable research has indicated that such mature gifted children do as well as their somewhat older peers if allowed to enter school early. Kindergarten and first grade can be considered a natural transition point where the actual acceleration is less noticed by other children. If the child is new to the class like everyone else, other children will tend not to question the placement.

### Grade Skipping

Grade skipping is what most people think of when acceleration is mentioned. It is often easier when done either early or late in a child's educational experience. Even though the sixth-to-seventh grade move is a natural transition point in districts having junior high programs, we do not highly recommend it as the moment for acceleration. The emotional stress of the seventh-grade transition is quite strong under ordinary circumstances, and adjusting to a totally new set of peers is probably an unnecessary extra burden.

Grade skipping for the mature child is best achieved in the fairly balanced learner who does not exhibit a marked deficit in a specific skill area. Caution needs to be exercised when the skip will place the child in the same grade or higher than an older sister or brother. In such instances, the family will need to make considerable preparation in anticipation of the move. Multiple grade skipping should be handled with even more preparation. Only a very small number of gifted children are suited for multiple skips, particularly at the elementary school level.

## Content Acceleration

Content or specific curriculum acceleration is fairly common as a form of academic advancement. This type of acceleration is flexible as a tool and is applicable to a large number of gifted and talented students. It comes in many guises. An administrator may allow his musically talented students a chance to study an instrument earlier than at the traditional beginning grade level. A child talented in math may be given seventh- or eighth-grade material in the elementary class-room, or an older child may participate in college-level courses at a local university.

Since 1971, Julian Stanley of Johns Hopkins University in Baltimore, Maryland, has run an acceleration program for mathematically gifted junior and senior high students. In the area of their specific talent these youths have been able to cover course work at their own pace. The experiment has proved very successful and the students as well as the educators seem pleased with the results.

Content acceleration is most successful in those areas where life experience is not a major factor, as in mathematics or science. People who work with musically talented students frequently point out that while their technical performance may be equal to that of an adult, they generally cannot render as good an interpretation of the music because of their lack of sophistication.

## Early Graduation

Another acceleration option is early graduation. This may be as dramatic as the junior high student who goes full-time to a local college or as ordinary as the youth who graduates six months to a year early. Early graduation presupposes that content acceleration has taken place in most academic areas. It will be rendered meaningless if the student does not have some plan for future educational endeavors.

## The Curriculum

The second component of a program is the curriculum—what the child is actually learning. Curriculum can be analyzed at either the concrete level—in terms of the text or materials being used—or the more abstract level of overall objectives.

The most vital aspect of curriculum development may be the program's statement of theoretical orientation and goals. Programs need to avoid isolated "cute" activities. They should be designed to foster individual excellence, not to entertain children with a bag of tricks. A good program for the gifted and talented may even contain some remedial aspects, especially when it serves handicapped or disadvantaged children. A program need not always adhere to one orientation faithfully over time. Some of the best model programs have incorporated sections of different theories at various points in their evolution. Do not be fooled, however, by a program that calls itself "eclectic"; on closer inspection it may turn out to lack a logical framework for its day-to-day functioning. Some programs seem to expound a sophisticated series of lessons but in actuality embody no idea of goals, accomplishment aims, or evaluation.

In order to help parents understand the orientation of their school district's actual or proposed program, we will discuss several models of curriculum theory. These are not the only acceptable models, but they typify some of the best-known ideas. The first three models—those of Bloom, Guilford, and Williams—are called cognitive (thinking) and affective (feeling) process theories. The fourth model, Renzulli's Triad, goes a step farther and should be examined separately. The discussion of all four theories is meant to be an introduction to a very abstract topic. We do not plan a detailed analysis of theory in this book. Parents who are interested in evaluating theory in more depth can consult the bibliography for books by the foregoing authors as well as works by Parnes, Rathe, and Taylor.

## Bloom's Taxonomy

In 1956, Benjamin Bloom presented his *Taxonomy of Educational Objectives* (68). A taxonomy is a grouping or classification system presented in levels as a hierarchy. Bloom's taxonomy grouped learning skills from the most concrete and basic stages to the highest and most abstract levels. Bloom was also involved in developing an affective taxonomy.

The first and most basic block of the Bloom cognitive taxonomy is called knowledge. The knowledge level deals with specifics such as terminology, facts, classifications, methods, and so on. Most of the present book also emphasizes the knowledge level of information. It can be said that you must acquire knowledge before you can go on to higher-level thinking skills. Unfortunately, too much of our attention has been focused on producing gifted information gatherers. Our children are all too familiar with tasks that begin with questions like "Name all the state capitals of the United States" or "Define cascade." At this stage the teacher directs and lectures while the child must memorize and respond to questions.

The second level of the taxonomy is called comprehension. This level suggests that the student understands the concepts being taught and can paraphrase, rearrange, and extend them. Typical questions are "Describe the causes of the American Revolution" or "Explain how a person becomes president of the United States." This is the stage at which the teacher is interested in demonstrating similarities and differences in situations. Children must be able to show that they understand a topic well enough to explain it to others.

The third level of the taxonomy is called application. This is the ability to make abstractions from information and then generalize from those abstractions to new situations. The teacher's role has become that of a facilitator and critic. The material is no longer merely understood and regurgitated; its principles are now applied to other problems.

The fourth taxonomy level is called analysis. This is the skill of examining a complex situation, discovering its important relationships, noting relevant detail, and deciding how all the parts work together to make the whole. Task analysis suggests pattern, sequence, and an organized, logical way of approaching situations. The teacher must merely guide and prod the student with appropriate clues at this level. The style becomes more Socratic; that is, the teacher questions to elicit an appraisal and solution to the problem.

The fifth taxonomy level is called synthesis and is equivalent to the creative act. The teacher continues as advisor, as critic, and as a sounding board for ideas, evaluating the student's plans and designs.

The final level is called evaluation, and is identical to what James Gallagher calls verification in creativity. During this stage the student is responsible for judging the adequacy and the value of his or her product. The teacher helps to clarify the child's assessment. This is the time for final modifications and for constructive criticism from the teacher.

Much time is spent in the regular classroom using the lowest levels of Bloom's taxonomy. Typically, a large percentage of children entering a special gifted and talented program have erratic analysis skills; this is because most of the previous problems presented to them were so circumscribed that the children obtained the answers without knowing how they solved them.

Bloom's taxonomy is frequently used to develop higher-level thinking skills. Many children whose programs use Bloom's taxonomy are able to label which level of thinking skill a task requires. The taxonomy helps them to understand what type of task they are dealing with and how sophisticated it is. This ability to understand how to think is a valuable tool for the children's future learning.

## Guilford's Structure of Intellect

In Chapter 3, we discussed Guilford's theory of the Structure of Intellect, often referred to as SOI. Instead of obtaining a total IQ estimate, SOI focuses on how individuals learn. It assumes that certain abilities can be taught, and it is therefore helpful in diagnosing learning styles in individual planning. SOI analysis can be made on a number of individual tests (such as the Stanford Binet, L-M and the Wechsler Intelligence Scale for Children–Revised [WISC-R]), or it can be performed from measures designed by Mary Meeker of the SOI Institute in California.

SOI is a rather complex model that may require several rereadings; Guilford's book *Way beyond the IQ* (39) is suggested for further clarification. In the model, each of the 120 factors making up intelligence is designated by what is called a "trigraph." The trigraph represents the three parts that con-

## Structure of Intellect Factors

| Factor | Letter | Example |
|---|---|---|
| Operation: Always the first trigraph letter | | |
| Cognition | C | Comprehension |
| Memory | M | Short- and long-term retrieval |
| Evaluation | E | Making judgments |
| Convergent | N | Exactness; finding the "best" solution |
| Divergent | D | Multiple or unique solutions |
| Content: Always the second trigraph letter | | |
| Figural | F | Perceptual material, i.e., auditory visual |
| Symbolic | S | Denotative signs, e.g., letters, numbers |
| Semantic | M | Abstract meanings attached to words |
| Behavioral | B | Human attitudes, moods |
| Products: Always the third letter of the trigraph | | |
| Units | U | Single pieces of information |
| Classes | C | Sets, e.g., fruits, animals |
| Relations | R | Comparing and contrasting, especially with concepts |
| Systems | S | Analysis of complex situations |
| Transformations | T | Flexibility, the ability to shift |
| Implications | I | Making hypotheses |

stitute each factor; each part is represented by one letter. The first letter of the trigraph designates the *Operation* or major intellectual process; the second letter designates the *Content* or type of material being processed; the third letter designates the *Product* or organizaton of the material processed. Let us use vocabulary as an example of a trigraph. Vocabulary would be coded CMU. The *C* stands for the operation of *Cognition* (comprehension), the *M* for *Semantic* content (abstract meaning generally attached to words), and the *U* for product *Units* (individual pieces of information). The translation of the code might be phrased "comprehension of word meanings." Vocabulary is just one example of the CMU type of skill.

Many SOI categories are equivalent to levels of Bloom's

taxonomy and are frequently used interchangeably. Some examples are: Cognition (Guilford) and Comprehension (Bloom); Systems (Guilford) and Analysis (Bloom); and Evaluation (Guilford) and Evaluation (Bloom). What distinguishes the Guilford model is its amount of detail, which breaks up the learning process more finely. The accompanying table, "Structure of Intellect Factors," summarizes the Guilford factors. It may help you recognize them if they are part of your school district's program.

## Williams's "Cube" Model

Frank E. Williams, an educational psychologist in Oregon, introduced his model in 1970. It is similar in some ways to Guilford's and was also designed to facilitate individual planning. The three dimensions of Williams's Cube Model are curriculum, teacher behavior, and pupil behavior.

Curriculum is the actual subject such as math or English. Teacher behavior is the teaching strategy, while pupil behavior is both the intellectual and the emotional style of the child.

Planning from this model is clear-cut, using various teaching strategies and encouraging the development of different pupil skills. In 1979 Williams stated in the *Gifted Child Quarterly* (103): "[The model] is based upon the importance of developing pupil-teacher interactions with the curriculum by dealing specifically with those cognitive and affective behaviors vitally responsible for encouraging and releasing creativity which have become well known from long standing research evidence."

## Renzulli's Enrichment Triad Model

In 1977 Joseph Renzulli, at the University of Connecticut, having examined what was being accomplished in gifted and talented education, stated in *The Enrichment Triad Model* (51) that many programs were not defensible; much of what was being done could not be justified as being beneficial for gifted and talented students alone. He therefore developed a model that would facilitate both the organization of gifted and talented education and program evaluation. As the name implies, there are three levels to the Renzulli model. The progression from level to level is not a one-way street, and students can go back and forth at any point depending on their particular needs. Level III activities are those that Renzulli feels should eventually be the main focus of a gifted and talented program.

Level I of the triad is called General Exploratory Experiences and contains a large element of enrichment. This can take the form of field trips or speakers. It can also encompass what Renzulli refers to as group exploration of a topic or an individual learning center where a student can examine a particular topic in depth. A large amount of time can also be spent in what children call "messing around." This may appear on the surface as wasting time, but it actually allows the student the opportunity to try out materials in a given field and to incubate ideas or develop the beginnings of a hypothesis.

Level II of the triad is called Group Training Activities. Here the teacher can employ cognitive and affective models like Bloom's or Guilford's to enhance learning skills. Activities at this level can involve such activities as brain teasers, simulations, and inquiry training. The important aspect of such tasks lies in the analysis of each problem and the emphasis on higher-level thinking skills wherever possible.

Level III of the triad is called individual and Small Group Investigation of Real Problems. Here much emphasis can be placed on creative outcomes, for example, publishing a book. Not all efforts are tied to actual production, however, and much time is also spent in content acceleration.

## Affective Training

Many educators complain that not enough emphasis is placed on social/emotional development in programs for the gifted and talented. In many sections of the country where gifted programs are barely getting off the ground, this is probably true. However, in areas where special programs have been in existence longer, attention to affective education is beginning to develop. Without a doubt, programs need to deal with the total child. Gifted and talented children need to be taught how to relate to others in the most positive manner possible. If they are going to work as a part of a professional team, or communicate their ideas, they need to be able to get along with others. Robbie's story illustrates this need.

Robbie was a highly verbal boy with an outstanding knowledge of many fields. He was dearly loved by the staff in his gifted and talented program but roundly hated by his peers. Robbie lacked common social sense. Never a discussion passed without his injecting a comment. He was usually right, but never received any encouragement from the other students. Robbie seemed oblivious to their scorn. He thought nothing of interrupting and correcting the statements of others. One day the class began a series of science projects. The teacher directed everyone to break up into groups, but no group was willing to let Robbie be a member. He was confused and upset, since he had no notion why no one would let him join. This presented the perfect opportunity for a class examination of the situation. Robbie's various annoying behaviors were pointed out and his classmates made some suggestions of things he could do to be better liked. Subsequently, Robbie has not totally changed his behavior. He is still not the best-liked child in the group. But he has managed to curb his bad habits and is now accepted in the team's work. To do this he has had to restrain his tendency to dominate every situation. Robbie will have to learn how to be a sensitive leader before the others will let him direct their ventures.

## The Teacher

The third component of a program for the gifted and talented—and probably the most important one—is the teacher. Teachers in gifted and talented programs must be as carefully chosen as they are for any other type of special education assignment. No amount of fancy equipment will cover up for unsympathetic, poorly prepared teachers.

When talking about who should teach the gifted, it is important to recall that we are dealing with human beings. Teachers are not pieces of sculpture that we can carve into some perfect design. An important tool in selecting teachers of the gifted and talented is plain old common sense. This would lead us to realize, for example, that a good teacher of the gifted must be a good teacher in general.

### Preparation and Certification

As late as 1978 only ten states had specific certification requirements for teachers of the gifted and talented. While a number of other states were considering requirements for such certification, standards were nowhere near uniform. Some of the states that began early to demand specific certification were Alabama, Georgia, Mississippi, North Dakota, North Carolona, and Virginia. It may be unreasonable, therefore, for you to expect that the teachers in your school district's program will be specially certified in gifted and talented education. If you have questions about certification requirements in your area, contact your state department of education.

While specific certification is still limited, there has been considerable growth in course work in teaching the gifted and talented. Options range from doctoral programs at schools like Columbia University, the University of Connecticut, and Purdue University, to single courses in a variety of settings. It is not unreasonable to expect that teachers selected from both within and outside the district to teach the gifted will have had some theoretical background. Because gifted education is in a constant state of flux, it would also seem reasonable that teachers continue to take workshops and courses in the field.

One method of teacher training might be to hire outside experts to run a series of in-service workshops or seminars. These workshops should not be what Joseph Renzulli calls one-shot "dog-and-pony shows." They must be part of an integrated whole if teachers are to gain a sense of logic and sequence and not just momentary inspiration.

## Teacher Characteristics

As we have already stated, the teacher of the gifted and talented needs to be a good teacher in general. However, some specific qualities are important as well.

The teacher is generally a facilitator and is not expected to be a jack-of-all-trades. Specialists should be employed where a child of extraordinary abilities requires considerable content acceleration. The teacher should not be easily upset by challenges from students on the content of lessons. A large percentage of gifted children are given to arguing every point and seeing every flaw in the arguments of the instructor. The thin-skinned teacher is doomed from the start. The teacher must also have considerable endurance, because the demands of gifted students tend to escalate as their skills develop. A third quality required is flexibility, whether in shifting the sequence of topics or altering content or teaching strategy.

The teacher must provide a model of the behavior that is wanted in the student. Those teachers who cannot be flexible have little chance of developing this trait in others. The teacher does not need to be a showperson. Many teachers in gifted programs have a less than dynamic presentation; however, their material is well thought out, and the students themselves are capable of bringing the topic to life.

# Student Selection Procedures

How do children in your school district become part of the gifted and talented program? Admittance may have been gained in any of a number of ways; there is no single entrance procedure for the gifted and talented as there would be for the educationally handicapped. Because so few states have stipulations on screening the gifted, school districts are generally free to follow their own inclinations. Let us discuss some of the options.

The simplest administration method is to establish group IQ and group achievement score cutoffs. Usually the achievement cutoff in such instances would be ninth stanine (or eighth at lowest). IQ score cutoffs would probably be set at 130 or higher (certainly not lower than 125). Using this method the children either qualify or they don't. Screening is simple because little time is involved in selection. There is not much argument with the decisions and all the children will be high achievers. Obviously, this type of program selects only able learners who test well in group situations and who appear fairly well balanced in their skills. It will not identify the talented, the disadvantaged, or children with uneven abilities. It will not be helpful in curriculum planning, because the selected students may not be quite as similar as they seem on first inspection.

A variation on this theme is to follow up the gross screening with individual intelligence testing. Usually this addition is not much more helpful because the test is again used as a single entity to sieve out inappropriately placed youngsters, but is not broken down for prescriptive reasons.

Another system is the use of what is called a matrix. A matrix is merely a mathematical formula in which different elements such as test scores and teacher recommendations are weighed. A weighed score is a score whose value may be doubled or tripled depending on the importance of the item the score represents in the matrix, such as achievement. The administrator generally decides what the minimal matrix total score should be for entrance into the program. Any child whose matrix total exceeds that cutoff score is in and any child whose matrix score comes out lower is out. Again, individual testing may follow the initial phase, but it functions in the same manner as it did in the previous method. The matrix method is troubled by the same difficulties as the simple cutoff method, except that the number of children that are overlooked is somewhat less. It still tends to discriminate against the talented and the disadvantaged.

Still another way for children to enter a program is through the "appeals" method. Here, the first part of the screening is by either the simple cutoff or the matrix method and will probably be called something like "direct entry." All those students who do not meet the initial program requirements but who are perceived by teachers or parents to be nonetheless gifted or talented can appeal the decision to a committee assigned to evaluate the cases on an individual basis. Where test scores are an issue, equivalent data may be submitted; these usually take the form of individual intelligence or achievement test scores. They can also include an individual assessment of creativity or personality. Equivalent data may be acquired through in-school individual testing or from outside professionals. This method allows the committee to decide what combination of skills the child shows and what chances of success he or she might have if admitted into the district's program. This is a much stronger system than the simple cutoff or matrix methods. Its only limitations are in the area of individual planning. A child may enter the program as an exception to the standard requirements, but generally nothing is individualized to help the child succeed. In such situations, once the child enters the program he or she must compete with the direct-entry children even if not starting off at the same academic level.

Probably the best method would be to model gifted and talented screening on the approach used in handicapped placement. This suggests several items. First, any individual evaluation should be done prior to presentation to a committee on the gifted and talented. The school staff should present data from multiple criteria suggesting why the student would benefit from placement in the program. They can include teacher nomination, peer and/or parent nomination, achievement, creativity, and intelligence test scores. In some cases they may involve an assessment of the talent area (such as music, dance, drama) by an expert in the field. There should be enough detail to give a total picture of the child. Equivalent data should be allowed to resolve any disagreement.

Using this approach, individual planning can result directly from the admissions information. When there is a standard requirement, the committee will know exactly why it is making an exception. Adjustments can be made in the child's program to accommodate any special needs.

The "Scale for Rating Behavioral Characteristics of Superior Students" is an illustration of a popular behavioral checklist developed by Renzulli and Hartman that can be employed in the nomination process. While there are some technical problems with the use of this checklist, many school districts have adapted it to fit their own requirements. The chances are that if the checklist is being used in your district, it has been altered from this original form.

### Scale for Rating Behavioral
### Characteristics of Superior Students*

*Directions: These scales are designed to obtain teacher estimates of a student's characteristics in the areas of learning, motivation, creativity, and leadership. The items are derived from the research literature dealing with characteristics of gifted and creative persons. It should be pointed out that a considerable amount of individual differences can be found within this population; and therefore, the profiles are likely to vary a great deal. Each item in the scales should be considered separately and should reflect the degree to which you have observed the presence or absence of each characteristic. Since the four dimensions of the instrument represent relatively different sets of behaviors, the scores obtained from the separate scales should not be summed to yield a total score. Please read the statements carefully and place an X in the appropriate place according to the following scales of values:*

*From L. S. Renzulli and R. K. Hartman, "Scale for Rating Behavioral Characteristics of Superior Students" *Exceptional Children* 38, no. 3 (1971):243–248. Copyright © 1971 by The Council for Exceptional Children. Reprinted with permission.

1. *If you have seldom or never observed this characteristic.*
2. *If you have observed this characteristic occasionally.*
3. *If you have observed this characteristic to a considerable degree.*
4. *If you have observed this characteristic almost all of the time.*

*Space has been provided following each item for your comments.*

*Scoring:* Separate scores for each of the three dimensions may be obtained as follows:

☐ *Add the total number of X's in each column to obtain the "Column Total."*

☐ *Multiply the Column Total by the "Weight" for each column to obtain the "Weighted Column Total."*

☐ *Sum the Weighted Column Totals across to obtain the "Score" for each dimension of the scale.*
   *Learning Characteristics* _____
   *Motivational Characteristics* _____
   *Creativity Characteristics* _____
   *Leadership Characteristics* _____

*PART I Learning Characteristics*     1    2    3    4

1. *Has unusually advanced vocabulary for age or grade level; uses terms in a meaningful way; has verbal behavior characterized by "richness" of expression, elaboration, and fluency. . . .*    ___  ___  ___  ___

2. *Possesses a large storehouse of information about a variety of topics (beyond the usual interests of youngsters his age). . . .*    ___  ___  ___  ___

3. *Has quick mastery and recall of factual information. . . .*    ___  ___  ___  ___

4. *Has rapid insight into cause-effect relationships; tries to discover the*

*how and why of things; asks
many provocative questions (as
distinct from informational or factual questions); wants to know
what makes things (or people)
"tick." . . .*                                        ___ ___ ___ ___

5. *Has a ready grasp of underlying
principles and can quickly make
valid generalizations about events,
people, or things; looks for similarities and differences in events,
people, or things. . . .*                             ___ ___ ___ ___

6. *Is a keen and alert observer; usually "sees more" or "gets more"
out of a story, film, etc. than
others. . . .*                                        ___ ___ ___ ___

7. *Reads a great deal on his own;
usually prefers adult level books;
does not avoid difficult material;
may show a preference for biogra-
phy, autobiography, encyclopedias,
and atlases. . . .*                                   ___ ___ ___ ___

8. *Tries to understand complicated
material by separating it into its
respective parts; reasons things out
for himself; sees logical and com-
mon sense answers. . . .*                             ___ ___ ___ ___

*Column Total*     ___ ___ ___ ___
*Weight*     ___ ___ ___ ___
*Weighted Column Total*     ___ ___ ___ ___
*Total*     _____

*PART II Motivational Characteristics*                 1   2   3   4

1. *Becomes absorbed and truly involved in certain topics or problems; is persistent in seeking task
completion. (It is sometimes difficult to get him to move on to
another topic.) . . .*                                ___ ___ ___ ___

2. Is easily bored with routine tasks. . . .    — — — —

3. Needs little external motivation to follow through in work that initially excites him. . . .    — — — —

4. Strives toward perfection; is self critical; is not easily satisfied with his own speed or products. . . .    — — — —

5. Prefers to work independently; requires little direction from teachers. . . .    — — — —

6. Is interested in many "adult" problems such as religion, politics, sex, race—more than usual for age level. . . .    — — — —

7. Often is self assertive (sometimes even aggressive); stubborn in his beliefs. . . .    — — — —

8. Likes to organize and bring structure to things, people, and situations. . . .    — — — —

9. Is quite concerned with right and wrong, good and bad; often evaluates and passes judgment on events, people, and things. . . .    — — — —

Column Total    — — — —

Weight    — — — —

Weighted Column Total    — — — —

Total    ————

---

*PART III Creativity Characteristics*    1  2  3  4

1. Displays a great deal of curiosity about many things; is constantly asking questions about anything and everything. . . .    — — — —

2. Generates a large number of ideas or solutions to problems and questions; often offers unusual ("way out"), unique, clever responses. . . .    — — — —

3. *Is uninhibited in expressions of opinion; is sometimes radical and spirited in disagreement; is tenacious. . . .*    —— —— —— ——

4. *Is a high risk taker; is adventurous and speculative. . . .*    —— —— —— ——

5. *Displays a good deal of intellectual playfulness; fantasizes; imagines ("I wonder what what would happen if . . . "); manipulates ideas (i.e., changes, elaborates upon them); is often concerned with adapting, improving, and modifying institutions, objects and systems. . . .*    —— —— —— ——

6. *Displays a keen sense of humor and sees humor in situations that may not appear to be humorous to others. . . .*    —— —— —— ——

7. *Is usually aware of his impulses and more open to the irrational in himself (freer expression of feminine interest for boys, greater than usual amount of independence for girls); shows emotional sensitivity. . . .*    —— —— —— ——

8. *Is sensitive to beauty; attends to aesthetic characteristics of things. . . .*    —— —— —— ——

9. *Is nonconforming; accepts disorder, is not interested in details; is individualistic; does not fear being different. . . .*    —— —— —— ——

10. *Criticizes constructively; is unwilling to accept authoritarian pronouncements without critical examination. . . .*    —— —— —— ——

*Column Total*    —— —— —— ——

*Weight*    —— —— —— ——

*Weighted Column Total*    —— —— —— ——

*Total*    ————

*PART IV Leadership Characteristics*                    *1    2    3    4*

1. *Carries responsibility well; can be counted on to do what he has promised and usually does it well. . . .*     —  —  —  —
2. *Is self confident with children his own age as well as adults; seems comfortable when asked to show his work to the class. . . .*     —  —  —  —
3. *Seems to be well liked by his classmates. . . .*     —  —  —  —
4. *Is cooperative with teacher and classmates; tends to avoid bickering and is generally easy to get along with. . . .*     —  —  —  —
5. *Can express himself well; has good verbal facility and is usually well understood. . . .*     —  —  —  —
6. *Adapts readily to new situations; is flexible in thought and action and does not seem disturbed when the normal routine is changed. . . .*     —  —  —  —
7. *Seems to enjoy being around other people; is sociable and prefers not to be alone. . . .*     —  —  —  —
8. *Tends to dominate others when they are around; generally directs the activity in which he is involved. . . .*     —  —  —  —
9. *Participates in most social activities connected with the school; can be counted on to be there if anyone is. . . .*     —  —  —  —
10. *Excels in athletic activities; is well coordinated and enjoys all sorts of athletic games. . . .*     —  —  —  —

*Column Total*          —  —  —  —
*Weight*          —  —  —  —
*Weighted Column Total*          —  —  —  —
*Total*          ————

### Who Should Be on the Committee?

The Committee on the Gifted and Talented should be made up of the program director (where there is one), at least one teacher of the gifted and talented, a school psychologist, at least one principal, and at least one parent of a child already in the program. The committee needs cross-membership representation similar to that of committees on the handicapped. Some people object to the presence of parents on the committee, claiming that parents are not expert enough to make placement decisions. They further object that parents should not be privy to private information concerning other people's youngsters because they may not keep the information confidential.

The answer to the first objection is that parents serving on committees on the handicapped do not function there as experts but as child/parent advocates. On the Committee on the Gifted and Talented parents should serve the same advocate function.

The second argument is handled even more easily. Case information can be number coded and identifying material on equivalent data blocked out so no one but the person with the master list and the presenting staff know who the child is. With this approach, confidentiality can be protected without losing the advantage of the child/parent advocate.

## "The Revolving Door"

How long should a child participate in a gifted and talented program? The question can be decided on the principle of the "revolving door," a term coined by Joseph Renzulli. In our adaptation of the principle, participation in a program need not be permanent, but on the other hand neither should there be a set time limit. As long as the child is benefiting from the placement he or she should be allowed to remain. Exit from the program should be a decision made jointly by parent, regular staff, and program staff. Children who drop out can always be renominated by the school staff should the need arise. If the program is good, children will receive continuous assessment of their efforts, enabling everyone involved to evaluate their current level of functioning.

# Summing Up

Equal education means appropriate education for the gifted and talented; such programming requires specialized curriculum planning.

School districts can use various methods for grouping and for curriculum development. These methods usually depend on district size, financial considerations, and commitment to special programming. The most effective grouping for the gifted and talented is the individualized classroom cluster with an in-house resource room. However, districts may come up with other groupings that are also suitable and that better fit their particular needs.

Curriculum must be well planned, using any of a number of alternative methods. Curriculum development needs to be based on some theoretical orientation. We have examined the major theories and offered some thoughts on affective education for the gifted.

Teacher selection is another important issue. Educators often joke that children learn in spite of the teacher. This is frequently true for the gifted and talented. However, good teachers can make a difference between mere absorption of facts and full development of a child's abilities.

Screening for special programs is often the most difficult part of any school district's gifted program. Administrators worry that parents may insist on their youngsters' participation in the program. However, administrators should be able to handle such challenges in a fair, understanding manner. This means making exceptions on occasions but also standing fast under heavy pressure when necessary and doing what is best for the particular child. The key is for both administrator and parent to be flexible and not defensive when dealing with each other.

# 6
# The Difficult Years: Adolescence

A dolescence—the years between childhood and adult-hood—is one of the major developmental stages in a person's life and probably one of the most conflictful. Besides the enormous physiological changes that take place, the adolescent has to cope with major psychological adjustments, making this period one of the most difficult stages of life a person has to pass through. In technological societies adolescence becomes a protracted period of dependence; educational options are expensive and drawn out, and the youngster often discovers that independence and self-sufficiency are difficult to attain.

## The Growth of Adolescents

Adolescence in our society must be viewed as both a physiological and a cultural development. The two do not completely coincide. Sexually, adolescents have reached adulthood in their ability to reproduce. Psychologically, however, most adolescents are not mature enough to behave and make decisions as adults. This gap between physical and psychological growth is probably due in large part to cultural factors. In the following pages we will investigate the various aspects of adolescence and assess what specific areas may be of concern to the gifted and talented.

## Physical Aspects

Puberty, the point at which sexual maturity begins, is considered to be the start of adolescence. Early puberty begins around ages 11–13 for girls and 12–15 for boys. This is the time when the most growth occurs in a person's height, though full height is not attained until age 16 for girls and after 18 for boys.

Girls both begin and end the physical changes of adolescence much earlier than boys. However, they tend to have greater difficulty accepting their change into womanhood than boys have in dealing with their transition into manhood. This may be related to their perception of the advantages they believe men to have both biologically and sociologically. In any case, today's adolescents appear to be physically maturing earlier than the youth of prior generations, possibly because of the more enriched nutrition that is afforded to children growing up today.

The physical aspects of adolescence exert a significant psychological impact. Because adolescents are very much concerned about being in step with their peers, they experience considerable anxiety over any developmental discrepancies they may display. For example, many teenagers grow disproportionately in comparison with other teens. The development of various parts of the body also progresses at highly different rates. The person who is short today may experience a spurt next week and find arms and legs unfamiliar and uncoordinated. Furthermore, these changes are difficult to predict, which can be disconcerting to the teenager who feels outstripped by peers.

Although these physiological irregularities are normal, individual adolescents do not see themselves as normal. They are highly self-critical. A girl who begins to mature early, for instance, may face difficult social problems and different decisions from her less mature peers. The same is true for boys who mature either early or late. Late-maturing boys, for example, may develop feelings of inadequacy, which usually follow them into adulthood.

Unfortunately, many parents are uncomfortable discussing physiological changes with their children. Even in what is often labeled a liberated society, jokes portraying this awkwardness are rampant. Yet, despite their frequently rebellious tendencies, teenagers look to their parents for support in this time of rapid change and emotional uncertainty. It can be upsetting to perceive that there are aspects of your person that are so distasteful that your parents shy away from dealing with them. Parents can help ease the burdens of adolescents by reaching out to them with honesty and by dealing openly with their questions and feelings as they arise.

## Cultural Aspects

Adolescence today is much different from what it was in primitive societies. In primitive societies there was, in essence, no adolescent period. The transition from childhood to adulthood was represented by a ritual known as the "rite of passage." These rites usually did not last more than a few weeks; once they were completed, the young people were considered to have assumed adult status. Their role as adults was perfectly clear.

Unfortunately, there is no such clear point of demarcation for youth in modern society. For us, adolescence—the transition from childhood to adult status—is a long-drawn-out period of trial. In our culture, emergence into adulthood has less to do with physiological changes than with cultural matters such as financial independence. Because the transition is a time of extended dependence, it is a very difficult period for everyone concerned. The rules governing teenagers' behavior become complex, and they are frequently resented by teenagers, who are eager for their dependency to end. In other cultures, after all, teenagers would already be beyond the control of their parents, and responsible for themselves.

The length of our adolescent period appears to be the result of our postindustrialized society, in which formal rites of passage have been eliminated and the child's entry into the adult work world considerably postponed. The actual event that marks the beginning of adulthood in our culture is quite vague. When does the adolescent turn into a mature adult? Should adults who are immature be considered adolescents? Because of this vagueness, the personal identity of adolescents is uncertain; they are neither children nor adults and are forced to live with considerable confusion. No wonder adolescents are emotional and rebellious!

## Parents and Their Adolescents

It is difficult for parents to accept the fact that their children are growing up. As mature as they seem physiologically, parents still see them as the helpless infants they first loved. They want to deny the reality of the children's changes, and as a result sometimes have trouble letting them go or allowing them to grow up emotionally. This difficulty arises in part from fears about how their own lives will change. If teenagers become mature enough to make their own decisions, the parents will experience a loss of control over them. Parents also may fear the children's moving out and leaving them alone at home in a so-called empty nest. Such growth requires parents to deal with themselves and develop new roles in life. Most parents do this rather successfully and are able to make the transition with a minimum of hard feelings on both sides. For other families the transition does not go quite so smoothly.

In one such family, the parents were so fearful of losing their only daughter, Ethel, to adulthood that they smothered her with all types of favors and material goods. Sadly, the young woman began to feel very pressured and frustrated, and she became quite depressed. She was uninterested in life in general and took to drinking heavily to avoid facing her problems. Psychotherapy helped her to attain independence from her parents, and they were finally able to let her go, developing a different lifestyle for themselves that did not include the presence of a young child.

Because of internal conflicts that both children and parents experience during adolescence, they often do not get along well. Parents have difficulty in coping with their teenagers, while most teenagers complain about their parents. This tug of war is entirely normal. Adolescence is the last great bid for independence. If the behavior of the teenager resembles that of the impossible two-year-olds, it is not without cause. Not since the harried parent had to cope with the toddler's tantrums has the child so striven for control of his or her own life. It would be surprising if conflicts did not occur; in fact, children who do not try to make the break for independence are a cause for concern.

However, some teenagers get along very well with their families and seem to experience minimal conflict. They have apparently identified well with their family's values and will eventually enter the adult world on good terms with their parents. If these young adults feel independent and can stand on their own feet, they will have successfully completed their transition into mature adulthood. However, even such cooperative young people need to have trusting parents who are able to let go. If they do not form an identity that is differentiated from the family, they may encounter difficulties in their adult lives. The essence of adolescence is the transition from childhood to independent, responsible adulthood, and teenagers who have not been able to successfully pull away from their families may behave like children throughout their later lives.

It is extremely important for parents to keep open communication with their teenagers. This is the key to ensuring a minimum of trouble for parents and children during this stressful period. Teens will do things that you do not approve of, but chances are that if your relationship is open and honest, the troubles they get into will be relatively minor. In addition, if teenagers feel that you are fair and that they can talk to you, they more than likely will come to you for advice in time of need. The child's early upbringing is crucial here, as the values and trust you instilled in the young child will pay off in adolescence. In the end, most teenagers adopt attitudes that are very similar to those of their parents.

It is important for parents to be aware of what their teenagers need and the difficulties they must go through. As discussed earlier, adolescents are torn by serious issues concerning their identity. On the one hand they are treated as children, while on the other hand they are expected to behave as mature and responsible adults. They desire independence from their parents and resent parental restraints, but financially they are still dependent on their parents, which only heightens their feelings of conflict. Physically, adolescents have powerful sexual urges, which society does not usually permit them to express. Although the risk of unwanted pregnancy is ever present, adolescents do not always act wisely. Many parents would like their teenagers to postpone sexual activity until adulthood, but the solutions they offer in the meantime are inadequate. This is another source of confusion and conflict between teenagers and parents.

## Peer Pressures

For adolescents, it is extremely important to be part of the peer group. This group of other teenagers begins to replace the family in importance to the teenager. Parents must learn to accept this displacement from the number-one position. In the child's thinking, the group now comes first, although the child may not always admit this overtly. This is a natural turn of events and is necessary if adolescents are to develop the feeling of independence they need. Positive peer relationships help in the maturing process. Parents should seek to encourage the child's participation in groups of youngsters with similar values and interests. Problems arise, however, when a teenager falls in with the "wrong crowd."

The wrong crowd is a group of adolescents who engage together in nonproductive behavior—behavior that is detrimental to themselves or to others. Teenagers who engage in antisocial behavior do so both because they find it rewarding and because it is a form of rebellion against the establishment. Like gifted underachievers, antisocial adolescents usually are not successful in situations valued by established society. Unfortunately, once teenagers reach this stage, it is difficult to pull them back to more acceptable views and behavior.

It has been estimated that about 60 percent of graduating high school seniors have tried marijuana, and about one-third of the high school populations have tried other drugs. One of the most difficult adolescents to reach is one who is using drugs. The danger in marijuana abuse is similar to that in alcohol abuse—use of the substances can become a way of life, a crutch to help one get through the everyday frustration and boredom of school and life in general. Teenagers who smoke marijuana heavily usually receive support for their behavior from their social environment—a group of friends who smoke also and whose lives are linked through the habit. Peer pressure makes breaking the marijuana habit difficult for those teenagers who want to stop smoking.

Alcohol abuse by adolescents also appears to be a growing problem. The use of alcohol, like that of marijuana, can be a way to ease the stresses of life and avoid dealing with uncomfortable feelings. Many teenage problem drinkers learn this behavior from alcoholic parents; studies have shown that about half the teenage alcoholics come from parents who are alcoholic themselves. The seriousness of the alcohol problem is becoming better recognized at the present time.

Teenagers who use alcohol and drugs to deal with frustrations may not have experienced enough success in dealing with the smaller frustrations of childhood. They may have been overprotected or encouraged to develop a dependent type of personality, which left them unable to solve their own problems.

Peer pressure also exerts a great deal of influence on teenage sexual activity. About 50 percent of the girls between 15 and 19 years of age have engaged in premarital sex, and the percentage may be rising. Many girls engage in sex because they want to be part of the crowd—it is a disgrace among some teenagers to be called a virgin. Boys, too, are under pressure to perform, although they have always been expected to use sex as part of their rite of passage, to prove their manhood.

However, most adolescents are not ready emotionally for a full sexual relationship. At a time when they should be learning to interact with many different people, it is a mistake for them to limit their social interactions by tying themselves to one partner because of sexual activities and thus failing to date other people. In addition, in the absence of the proper information and birth control devices, sexual activity involves the danger of pregnancy; approximately one out of every ten teenage girls becomes pregnant each year. The difficulties for a teenage girl of raising a child when she herself has barely completed childhood can have detrimental effects both on her offspring and on her own growth. Unfortunately, many teenagers are unprepared for responsible sexual activity because their parents have been reluctant to deal with the topic. In-school programs are generally limited to the mechanics of reproduction and fail to deal with value-laden issues.

### Living in the Postindustrial World

Part of the confusion adolescents experience has to do with the difficulty adults have in handling their own lives. Many adults, struggling to figure out what is appropriate behavior for themselves, fail to offer adolescents the models of mature behavior they need. The lack of adequate models places an undesirable burden on teenagers today. In addition, we are living through times of economic difficulty in which adults must spend a great deal of time and energy working just to make ends meet. This leaves them with little time to spend with their children. Society has not yet developed means to fill the gap left in the home by working parents, so that many children are left with the burden of raising themselves.

Economic difficulties also affect teenagers directly. Earning money at a job would help to satisfy their need for independence and gain them desirable status in the adult world. Unfortunately, there are not enough jobs to go around. This leaves some teenagers with no other options except to hang out, a situation that breeds a sense of purposelessness and alienation from society and can lead to antisocial behavior. The confusion and resentment present in many adolescents become understandable when we see how little society provides them in the way of meaningful direction, economic opportunity, or adults to model and direct their time. It is no wonder that teenagers cannot wait to become accepted as adults even though they have less than a clear notion of how to go about it.

## Gifted Adolescents

Gifted and talented adolescents have to deal with the same difficulties that confront their peers. However, their special attributes add an extra complication. One gifted boy recently commented that it was hard to deal with the other kids in junior high school because they did not treat the kids in the honors program as "human." He had to cope with being different from his peers as well as with all the stresses of growing up.

Although gifted and talented teenagers have an additional set of unique problems, they also enjoy some advantages as well. Because they are sensitive and have more insight into their lives, they are able to perceive and verbalize what is going on. If they have conflict with the peer group, they can look beyond it. They have other alternatives to turn to. A case illustration will demonstrate what we mean.

Elisa was a typical 16-year-old who enjoyed many of the things typical 16-year-old girls do. She had a good relationship with her parents and still shared many activities with them. Her school work was excellent and she received A's in all her subjects. She belonged to various school clubs and could always be counted on to do work for extra credit.

Elisa had only one real friend, however, though she considered some of the girls nodding acquaintances. She did not date boys regularly. Although she was verbally fluent, she was not popular with her classmates. In some respects she did not have time for them because she was so involved with her schoolwork and with personal activities such as horseback riding, photography, wood carving, and reading. Elisa seemed content to spend much of her time alone. She admitted that she sometimes wished she had more friends and could go out on dates, but she was frustrated by efforts to participate in a more active social life. Elisa was not interested in many of the things that excited the other girls. She did not like just to hang out and she found that the other girls were rarely interested in discussing topics she favored. For her part, she found most of their conversations trite and boring. Although she had tried, she was not successful at gaining more friends. In the end, she simply gave up and decided that her one good friend was sufficient. Now, as she put it, "I try to do things that interest me and make the most I can of all situations."

Elisa, who is academically gifted, knew why she did not have more friends, but she could not—as many parents and educators falsely believed she naturally would—figure out how to deal with her conflict and develop more socially accepted behavior.

Many gifted and talented adolescents feel more comfortable pursuing academic and related areas than competing in the social arena. Even when they are involved in activities such as music, they experience social difficulties. Alan, for example, began to study the violin in elementary school, but by the time he had entered junior high, he was becoming uneasy with the instrument. He received many jibes that "real men" did not play "sissy" instruments; he said that brass was in and string instruments were out. He denied that there was peer pressure not to perform well, but the instrument teacher reported that it was a continual battle to keep the most talented students at their high level of excellence. Alan, like many others, apparently sought to produce an average performance so that he would be more accepted by his peers. This conflict over his musical ability was so severe during his first year of junior high school that for a time Alan refused to play the violin; and he wanted no part of the summer camp he had attended for many years, with its emphasis on musical, artistic, literary, and dramatic talents. With the aid of therapy, however, Alan's mother, at her wits end, learned to be supportive and wait out the difficult period, while Alan learned to accept being different. Recently the two spent the day in the city with Alan's music teacher, selecting a better-quality violin. Instead of running away from his musical talent, Alan is now talking about music as a career and has been thinking about starting a second instrument.

Alan is now in the ninth grade. Socially, he states that his most difficult moments are in relating to girls. He would like to date, but says he has little in common with girls who are not gifted; he finds little to talk about with girls who are not involved in music or who don't desire academic achievement.

Like Alan in junior high school, those gifted adolescents who choose to become more popular with the group may find themselves compromising their own talents in order to belong. Elisa, who was not willing to do this, is an unusual case, since many gifted girls choose to pursue the avenue of popularity, relinquishing their academic and career interests. Parents may need to devote special encouragement to their gifted daughters to help them develop both social and academic skills so that they can have the best of both worlds.

Studies have shown that gifted students have lower expectations for success in their social endeavors than in their academic interests. Two hypotheses have been proposed to account for this discrepancy. One is that gifted students focus more attention on academic skills because they are encouraged to do so by significant adults in their life. Alan, for example, complained during seventh grade that when he made several friends, his parents—always unhappy that he had few friends—began to harangue him that he was neglecting his schoolwork. Alan felt trapped; he did not know what his parents really wanted from him.

Parents should be wary about overemphasizing academic achievement to the detriment of important social areas. Many gifted individuals appear to the world at large as socially inept because they have not had many varied experiences; they have not learned how to communicate with other people. Such teens often have overbearing, overconcerned parents who would not let the child develop independence; the parents rightfully fostered academic growth, but failed to help the child develop other abilities.

A second hypothesis, and this is true for both Elisa and Alan, is that acceptance by the peer group requires the individual to be as similar to the others as possible; those who are different are teased and shunned by their peers. The fact is that gifted and talented adolescents are different in many ways from their contemporaries and may encounter a difficult time finding their niche in adolescent society.

Reports from gifted adults indicate similar findings. These adults recall that their worst years in school were during the junior and senior high period. Not only was the academic program boring, but they found themselves alienated from their classmates; their social adjustment was awkward and uncomfortable. They recall that their best experiences were in college, where they felt academically challenged and dealt with classmates of similar maturity and interests.

Programs for the gifted and talented at the secondary level have to be a lot more than just academics. Schools need to spend more time on individual attention and less time on repetitive work, giving more attention to teaching decision making, increasing counseling services, and providing more chances for creativity and acceleration. Group counseling sessions led by trained personnel are needed, especially on the high school level, for gifted and nongifted teens as well. These groups should center around specific social and interpersonal problems encountered by all types of students. Groups for teachers would also be worthwhile to help them deal with their feelings about exceptional children and to aid them in working more effectively with the gifted and talented.

Finally, for programs to be most effective, groups for administrators are also needed. Most administrators shy away from programs that may be controversial. By encouraging them to partake in consciousness-raising programs concerning the exceptional child, we are ensuring more successful programs as well as adding the opportunity for developing new and exciting ideas.

## Facades

Many gifted children have a facility for elaborate, highly developed forms of speech. A result of this verbal glibness in the adolescent is that the listener believes the individual to be older and more mature than he or she really is. However, verbal facility is often a mask for an insecure youth, who may be hiding conflicts behind a verbal haze. The gifted child's appearance of maturity keeps parents and other adults from fully realizing the problems the child may be experiencing. People sometimes expect too much from the gifted adolescent. They forget that someone of 13 or 15 cannot produce the feelings or behavior of a college student. Such erroneous expectations often give rise to conflict between parents and teenager; parents react in shock that the youth could suddenly turn so irresponsible, when in fact the behavior may simply be typical of the age group. Let us examine two examples.

Larry was the second of four children and was considered intellectually gifted. His mother describes him as having the most common sense of his siblings. Larry was always responsible and was very protective of his sisters. One day, when he was in junior high school, he and a friend became involved in a playful mock fight. Before long they were chucking rocks at each other. Larry was hit in the head and came home with a large lump. His mother was aghast. She wondered how good, responsible Larry could become involved in such dangerous behavior. She forgot that gifted children are just as prone as others to get carried away.

Cindy's case is another typical instance of parents' overestimating their adolescent's maturity level. Cindy is a capable student who was always involved in mature interests. When she was preparing for college, she worked long hours to accumulate money so that she could relieve her parents of the financial burden. Her brothers and sister all looked to her as a leader and her classmates frequently came to her for help with their problems. This is where Cindy's conflict was. She felt that no one was willing to be her confidant. Everyone, including her parents, seemed to think she had perfect sense and no conflicts.

Just before college, Cindy broke up with her boyfriend. While she was not ready for another relationship, her friends pressured her into going out on a date with another boy. Her parents also took her surface calm for granted and encouraged her to go out. Throughout the date, Cindy was very nervous and uncomfortable. In order to deal with the social situation, she drank too much wine, and by the end of the evening she was drunk, something that had never happened to her before. Her parents were awake when she returned home, and it is difficult to say who was more upset by her condition, she or they. In the midst of their remonstrations, Cindy complained that she never would have gotten drunk if she had not been pushed into going out on the unwanted date. Now, certainly Cindy's behavior was her own responsibility. Still, everyone had taken her surface calm at face value; had they understood that she had feelings and reactions the same as theirs, they might not have pressured her into an uncomfortable situation.

# Working Hard for the First Time

A common complaint from parents of the gifted is that their children never have to extend themselves to produce good-quality work. They have frequently breezed through elementary school, studying little, taking few notes and generally underutilizing their abilities. Reality may set in either at the secondary school level or during the first year of college. Vastly altered demands catch the adolescent unprepared, and parents are frequently appalled at how much difficulty the child gets into. Again, let us look at some real-life experiences of gifted adolescents.

Alan had always been a remarkable child. At 15 months of age, he said to his pediatrician, "What took you so long? Hurry up and just weigh and measure me." He romped through elementary school at the top of his class, and was placed in the honors track in junior high school. Even there, he was able to get by with minimal effort. That is, until the science competition came up.

Alan decided to do a learning experiment comparing the abilities of various rodents. Although it was a complex topic, he went no further than to get some books from the local library and read up on learning theory. His parents tried to prod him into further action, but to little avail.

Two weeks before the contest, Alan went into a whirl of activity. He completed the maze, ran the animals, and slapped together the results into a neat but sketchy summary. He told his parents he planned to ad lib the oral presentation. While they were less than pleased, they realized they could not convince him of his underestimation of the competition. They decided to let the contest judges take care of him.

Alan went through with his plan, and talked about the topic off the top of his head. His presentation was good, though it was far from complete. Disregarding the fact that other students were better prepared, Alan clearly expected to take top honors that night. He was irate when he received only a third place in his division.

It was only after considerable discussion with his parents that Alan acknowledged where the fault really lay. For the county runoff, he decided to revamp his work and went into the second competition with a vastly improved presentation. It was still far below the quality that he could have produced, but his parents were pleased that he had put forth the effort to redo it. Alan was very happy to have his work rewarded with a better prize in this more demanding contest. Alan had met reality. If he wanted to be tops in the competition, he was going to have to work harder. Last-minute preparation was out.

Alan was fortunate to have learned this lesson early. Beth was not so fortunate. She did not see academic reality until the end of her freshman year of college. Beth, like Alan, had always been a top student. She was in an honors track and on the surface seemed to be working very hard. In high school she took four years of math and science, four years of two foreign languages, one year of another, and English and social studies. She received a high rating on the advanced-credit English exam as well as three scholarships to college. She was looking forward to a highly successful time after high school. Prior to attending the college, Beth and her mother saw a college guidance counselor to set up her program. Based on her scores and past history, they planned a very demanding program for her. Unfortunately, no one—neither Beth, nor her mother, nor the counselor—took into account the transition adolescents must make in their first year of college. Her program was overambitious and Beth found herself swamped with work.

Beth had to cope with several science courses, sophomore English, and several other sophisticated classes including an experimental social studies course. She went into a tailspin, almost flunked out, and lost one of her scholarships. It took her the balance of her college career to pull herself together and get good grades. She simply was not prepared to make good judgments about how much time her course work would consume or how heavy a program she should carry.

Beth's case is not unique. For some students, the freshman year of college is disastrous. The problems arise from poor work habits, low academic demands in high school, a highly pressured college situation, and poor judgment about how much pressure a new college student is capable of dealing with. All in all, the initial college experience is frequently not the way adolescents have pictured it, and may not turn out to be the rewarding situation many of them have expected.

## What is Advanced Placement?

Advanced placement is a special program run in conjunction with the College Entrance Examination Board. It may or may not be considered part of an honors program at the high school level. It is a form of content acceleration in which students have the chance to discover what a college level course is like while they are still in high school. The courses are given in a variety of subjects and at the end of the year the student is eligible to take an exam that is marked by a committee outside the high school. Students whose performances are highly rated may be granted college credit in the subjects they have taken. Unfortunately, there is no unified college policy on granting credit. If your adolescent is interested in advance placement courses, have him consult the guidance counselor as to which courses are available in your high school. Descriptions of the various courses are available at a small cost from College Board Publications Orders, Box 2815, Princeton, New Jersey 08541. When it comes time to apply to college, be sure to inquire about the school's individual policies with respect to advanced standing.

## Honors or Enriched?

Parents frequently ask how honors classes differ from enriched classes, particularly when they occur in the same school. Typically, honors classes are considered more demanding than enriched programs. Children placed in enriched programs, while they are performing at an above-average level, are not considered able to cope with the pressure and increased work load of honors.

In some school districts, however, honors and enriched classes are one and the same thing. If in doubt, inquire about the program differences at the secondary level in your school. Honors programs are at their best when students participate only in those classes where accelerated and challenging content is appropriate to their skills. These decisions should be based on concrete data for *each individual* and not on generalizations such as "math is not a girl's best subject." Unless early judgments are formed on a case-by-case basis, students will not be provided with appropriate programs.

Good elementary school gifted and talented programs are very helpful in this respect. If skills are assessed at the elementary level and are followed up during the years the child participates in the program, the secondary schools will benefit. The junior and senior high schools will be able to apply the data to the planning of the student's courses.

# Career Education

For the gifted or talented adolescent, making career choices will probably be more difficult than anyone expects. When children are young they identify with a number of highly visible work roles such as firefighter or police officer. Yet there is no systematic way for youth to "try out" various occupations. The gifted or talented youth is frequently overwhelmed with choices and would benefit from extensive guidance on career components and options. Part of the difficulty is resolving conflicts between the student's desires and abilities for certain types of work and the needs of society, which are constantly shifting.

Career education can be handled in a number of ways. One approach is to have community members from a variety of occupations work with students in the gifted and talented program. Not only can they explore current options but they can examine future possibilities. In our technological world, vocational choices may alter radically with changing social demands. Gifted and talented youth must be ready to develop their own careers during this shifting of priorities. It may be useful for them to hypothesize where technology is changing careers and what characteristics the new careers will demand. Gifted and talented youth need to understand that change is extremely rapid today and that they must be ready to shift their vocational plans as the need arises. Attention can be given to the sciences and other specific areas so that the adolescent can gauge where the change will be most rapid and how dramatic it may be. Stress may also be placed on how the boundaries that have traditionally separated different vocations are disintegrating, leading to new fields that are combinations of several old ones.

Another method for developing career choices is to allow the adolescent to spend a day with various professionals. For some medical groups this has been a common practice for many years. Spending a day with a doctor, speech therapist, or computer specialist will demonstrate to youth the realities of the work world. Certainly people want to be involved in a job that they find pleasurable, but it is also helpful to realize that day-to-day work is often less than glamorous.

A third approach expands on the theme of real-life experience. Here adolescents spend an extended amount of time working in community jobs allied to their vocational interests.

An ambitious program may attempt to integrate all three of these techniques. The more options adolescents consider, the more likely they are to discover what areas fit best with their skills. Paper-and-pencil tests of occupational interests, which are often bland and limited in scope, supply the adolescent with very little career guidance. With improvements in our secondary programs we can work to replace these shallow measures with meaningful experiences.

## Getting Set for College

Do not let your children fool themselves regarding the importance of the last year of high school. It is not something to waste. If they have not opted for some form of early graduation, they should focus on developing their skills during the senior year. Colleges are less than impressed with students who drift through the last year of high school; bad habits formed then will show up when the student enters college. Encourage your children to spend time in good-quality courses that will add merit to their applications. If the chance is offered, they might consider enrolling in classes that develop writing ability. Many college freshmen are overwhelmed by the demands for written assignments and, sadly, often discover that their skills are not up to the challenge.

## Summing Up

Out of the turmoil of a conflict-ridden period emerges a person who, for better or for worse, must face the responsibility of adulthood. This is when parenting ceases, for all practical purposes, and when young adults are left to fend for themselves—just as the bear chases her cub up a tree. The end of adolescence does not mean that children stop growing, nor for that matter do parents. It means that they can find their own directions as adults, as we have managed to find ours. It does not prevent us from occasionally offering advice nor does it suggest that our children can't approach us for advice. We must realize, though, that the final decisions children make should be theirs and that they are standing on their own. This is, in a nutshell, what parenting is all about.

Gifted teenagers face the same challenges and decisions as their peers. They still have much growing to do emotionally. In fact, such growth never ends. Gifted individuals have to deal with whatever course of action they lay out for themselves, a course that parents have helped to plan with them. As they go on their course, choose a mate, and have children of their own, the cycle continues. We can only hope that a lot of the kinks are worked out while we as parents have our chance to carry the ball. If not, it will be up to our children to try to make things better for their children.

Education of the gifted does not end with adolescence. Gifted adults can continue their education by feeding themselves on the knowledge the world has to offer. Giftedness, to be of value, must be utilized; otherwise it will wither and die.

# 7
# The Other Gifted

T he term "other" gifted refers to those gifted and talented children and adults who are significantly different from the typical gifted population. The "typical" gifted child is often pictured to be a white, middle- to upper-class, high-achieving male. Everyone else in the gifted classification can be considered other. It is felt that the other gifted are in some way at a disadvantage when compared with the typical gifted or talented child. They have to overcome some barrier, whether it is a disability they possess or a restriction society imposes on them. Specialists in gifted and talented education have felt that once the other gifted overcome these barriers they will be able to work to their full potential and contribute something of merit to themselves and to society.

The other gifted we will explore are the female gifted; the culturally different and disadvantaged gifted (including black, Spanish-speaking, Native American, and Asian); and the handicapped gifted (those gifted and talented individuals with learning, physical, or emotional handicaps). These are the groups of gifted and talented persons whose potential is generally being overlooked and underutilized.

## Women as Disadvantaged

Compared with the gifted man, the gifted woman in our society has been largely left by the wayside and not encouraged to move on to higher achievement. This plight of the gifted female student has been allowed to continue by both men and women. Many experts feel that the lack of encouragement for the gifted female child is often caused by the socialization process that takes place in today's world.

The traditional attitude has been that it is not as important for girls to be high achievers or to use their gifts and talents as it is for boys to do so. This attitude has been slowly changing over the years due to the consciousness-raising efforts of many women's groups as well as other alterations in social mores and technology. These additional changes have occurred as women have been forced to become more independent and self-sufficient—because of both economic pressures and the easing of the obligation to marry or have children. These have meant that women must now depend on themselves more than ever before. Consequently, they must develop and use their intellectual skills as tools in making a living, and they must seek status and success using the same rules that apply to men.

Although these changes in women's style of living are going on right now in our country, girls in school are still subject to a set of attitudes toward sexual roles that is largely unchanged. Girls are encouraged to behave in what are considered traditional "feminine" ways, including submissiveness, dependency and development of interests centered in home activities and child rearing. Unfortunately, these attitudes are not reinforced solely by men. Many women themselves feel that this is still the proper way for them to behave. In fact, many a girl rationalizes that she can always fall back on getting married and being dependent on a man if she can't cope with the demands of a career. Such a girl is only fooling herself, however; in a world where the most traditional institution of all, marriage, is changing so radically, women no longer can fall back on traditional behaviors.

### Roles

It is theorized that traditional attitudes toward sex roles are the result of a process akin to brainwashing, to which girls are exposed right from birth. This consists of more than just pink rooms and doll houses. Women's thinking is shaped by the entire manner in which the world is presented to them. One must remember that roles are really a set of complementary expectations that dictate how a person will interact with others. People have more than one role at a time, and some roles are only vaguely defined. Role conflict arises when the different roles are contradictory or mutually exclusive; this happens especially when the roles are ambiguous and frustrating. To resolve the conflict, a person may have to choose between the different roles. Because negative sanctions are attached to nonconformity, the more ambiguous a role is, the more threatening it is to the individual. For women there are many negative sanctions attached to choosing achievement-oriented roles.

Traditional feminine role values are often seen to be a product of the middle class, which rigidly separates male-female sex roles and is intolerant of a diversity of values in society as a whole. The person's decisions are dictated by an external authority that supplies simple, morally proper definitions of what is required in each situation. Sex-role identification is probably the most heavily reinforced of all role behavior; it assumes awareness if not necessarily acceptance of traditionally prescribed sex-role behaviors.

## How Girls Acquire Roles

Sex-role identification, like other forms of identification, is acquired through modeling. The child is encouraged by the parent to learn socially correct role behavior, which is then markedly reinforced by individuals outside the home. Roles are also reinforced by the use of parental love as a reward for proper behavior. A third factor in learning appropriate sex-role behavior is the parents' success at their respective roles, which are then observed and imitated by the child of the same sex. The child tries out the parent's role and is bolstered by the parent's elation over his or her success. In the matter of achievement, for example, it has been surmised that one reason girls tend to switch goals at the college level is that their parents no longer applaud achievement but reinforce more traditional role expectations.

How early are children aware of expected role behavior? Research has shown that as early as elementary school children see the father as stronger, smarter, and the "boss." Those girls who go on to positive achievement and worldly success have parents who supported them in their role choices and gave them the options of choosing activities identified with either sex. Where such opportunities are lacking, sex roles that have been traditionally reinforced by society at large are difficult to shed. Research indicates that women nearing the end of their schooling persist in selecting occupational categories defined as feminine.

Since girls have not been groomed for educational achievement they seem to take a back seat to boys in the secondary schools. This is ironic because in the early elementary grades girls generally excel. A number of reasons have been proposed for the early school success of girls, including conformity to discipline, advanced language skills, and a lesser need than boys to learn through gross motor exploration. By the secondary level, however, girls no longer dominate the classroom. Boys are more focused and less active than in the earlier grades; they are perceived as more cooperative and are reinforced for achievement, more than girls are. Girls have become less assertive than boys in class. They also encounter many more male teachers who may not expect as much achievement from them. The gifted girl suffers from this situation even more than her less-talented peers.

It is a sad fact that the parents of gifted and talented girls often do not encourage them to achieve and to pursue professional careers. For example, the parents of boys often discuss careers in the sciences, medicine, and mathematics with their sons. On the other hand, the parents of girls usually give less thought to their future plans. When the parents of gifted girls do plan with their daughters they often unconsciously nudge them toward more traditionally feminine careers.

One such case comes to mind of two gifted siblings, Peter and his younger sister, Clara. Peter was encouraged to go to college and to pursue a career in medicine. On the other hand, Clara, whose tested level of ability was very similar to his and who in fact had a higher verbal IQ than he did, was encouraged to stay at home and pursue mostly social interests. She did win a scholarship to college but chose to work as a typist in a large office. She eventually married someone with little achievement orientation himself and later found herself dissatisfied with both her marriage and her lot in life.

Examples like this are more common than you might expect and may explain why many women go back to school when their children get older. These are often highly intelligent women who enjoyed their role as homemaker but then decided to try to challenges of the outside world, breaking out of the traditional role to which they had assigned themselves in earlier years. Lewis Terman, who did considerable long-term research on gifted individuals, was interested in the percentage of persons who would wish to switch roles with their spouse. His investigation of over 1,000 individuals indicated that 42 percent of the women wished for opposite sex roles. Research by other investigators has shown that the percentage of women wishing to switch roles ranged from 34 percent to 61 percent. Many of the women who actually seek to switch roles and pursue professional careers find that their lack of feelings of self-worth is the hindrance. They are not comfortable with the level of competitiveness required, and the lack of confidence they have in their abilities is probably a very real obstacle to their success.

## The Conflict between Achievement Orientation and Tradition

It has been proposed that the requirements necessary for a woman to be considered feminine are contrary to the requirements for successful achievement. Successful achievement requires aggressiveness and competitiveness, which are definitely not in agreement with traditional feminine characteristics. It has been felt that women are reinforced against desiring achievement-related goals, through biased stereotyping, social ostracism, and unequal and inferior rewards. Thus, success for a woman has negative consequences and women may fear and avoid success. To become aggressive and competitive may be uncomfortable for women because they have been conditioned to develop different personality traits. Women fear that their achievement may lead to heterosexual conflicts and that their spouses and male friends may reject them. However, women who accept their traditional place may be presenting a facade to the world. It has been hypothesized that underneath, many of them are really very hostile; because their potential and interests are unfulfilled, they experience frustration, bitterness, and confusion.

Terman noted these negative reactions to achievement of gifted women of the generation now in their 60s and 70s. His research indicated that those women who did not go to college or who did not complete their schooling made a less satisfactory adjustment than the rest of the female sample. His findings may still be applicable today.

In 1975 one of the present authors was investigating role perception and marital adjustment in a sample of highly intelligent couples. In the process of the study the spouses took an abbreviated form of the Wechsler Adult Intelligence Scale. Each test subject was then asked to estimate his/her own and his/her spouse's performance on the test. The data had indicated that men and women taken as a group had an almost identical performance on the intelligence measure. The wives, however, consistently saw their husbands as more intelligent than they actually were. The husbands, on the other hand, were quite realistic in rating both their own and their wives' test scores. The subjects of this study had taken, among other measures, an estimate of how traditional their role perceptions were. Women with a more traditional score on the role-perception measure were more likely to rate themselves poorly and their spouses well than were other women in the study. It is also noteworthy that those bright women with a lower educational level tended to have a poorer marital adjustment.

The implication of the research is that programs for the gifted and talented must take into consideration the role conflicts of gifted women. Gifted and talented adolescents in particular need to see successful achieving women as models for their own behavior. They need staff members to identify with, especially in subject areas traditionally considered masculine. Educators must identify those girls who have unusual potential in traditionally masculine areas and make an active effort to foster those skills. It is useless to debate how much of such skills is biologically based. Even if what we are doing is identifying the exceptions to the rule, the staff of a specialized program should strive to preserve those exceptions. As mentioned in earlier chapters, individualized profiles are needed to help us better direct our gifted and talented female students. And when we deal with career education for gifted women we must also be aware of our own biases. Too many counselors are guilty of steering women into traditional professions without even realizing that they are doing so.

# Culturally Different Versus Disadvantaged

John Gowan, in *The First National Conference on the Disadvantaged Gifted (72)*, defined the disadvantaged child as one "being reared by *poor, lower* class native parents out of the cultural mainstream." They often do not score well on traditional tests because the tests favor the middle- and upper-class and because the childrens' disadvantaged status distorts the test profiles in the same manner that severe emotional problems distort scores, that is, by depressing the high or peak performance.

We must be cautious in equating the culturally different with the disadvantaged, however. Members of the predominant American cultural group seem fond of saying that anyone other than themselves is deprived, which expresses a negative view of ethnicity. Different does not necessarily mean disadvantaged. For example, not all Spanish-speaking people are disadvantaged, but many poor whites are clearly so. We must avoid using stereotypes of cultural groups and instead see that disadvantage is directly related to social and economic class. Furthermore, it is the stereotype of a cultural subgroup that helps to alienate its members from the mainstream and contributes to the difficulty in identifying gifted and talented minority youngsters. Because of the attitudes of the mainstream culture, minority children feel rejected and inadequate. You cannot expect to obtain a truly accurate ability estimate from a frustrated, angry child who has little confidence and an even lower self-image. We must take all the diverse cultural and socioeconomic factors into account when we begin to plan for both the disadvantaged and the culturally different gifted and talented youngsters.

## The Black and Hispanic Minorities

It is frequently noted that it is difficult to identify gifted or talented black and Spanish-speaking children using white middle-class standards. While there are numerous reasons for this difficulty, probably the most dominant factor is language.

In lower-class black and Hispanic cultures children are trapped by a language barrier that they must overcome to be successful in the mainstream culture. These youngsters fail to do well in school and on testing because they do not use language the way the middle-to-upper-class white person does. (This factor of poor language skills is also a characteristic of lower-class white pupils.) The emphasis in our school curriculum is on verbal skills and on the form of English used in the middle-class home. This form of language is set up in a logical, sequential fashion, with a beginning and ending and a fairly clear meaning, and it encourages children to think in this fashion. The language is characterized by more questioning and less commanding behavior. It allows children to think more independently and to reach larger numbers of their own conclusions.

In homes of the lower class, on the other hand, whether black, Hispanic, or white, there is more control associated with language. The black, Spanish-speaking, or poor-white parent will offer a child a predetermined solution with few alternatives for consideration. Thus children from these groups, regardless of their innate potential, are at a disadvantage in the development of skills, especially verbal ones.

Even in nonverbal abilities, with the exception of gross motor skills, lower-class children are at a disadvantage. They are not exposed to as many or as varied games, toys, and developmental paraphernalia as their middle-class counterparts. They not only miss the fine motor perceptual skills that may be a part of these games and other opportunities, but also do not get the exposure to the nonverbal thinking abilities and organizational skills that may be entailed. They often do not have the opportunities of travel and exposure to a stimulating environment. These children are at a disadvantage in terms of thinking approaches and information valued by the predominant culture when they enter school. Many minority youngsters who may be gifted or talented are overlooked in the selection process because they may be doing just average or slightly above average work in the classroom.

Spanish-speaking children face yet another problem and that is that their language is completely different. Bilingual children have frequently been known to have problems in school. They become confused with the two languages. They may be able to communicate in English but have difficulties at the conceptual level of the language. They are therefore at a disadvantage when compared with their middle-class English-speaking counterparts. Hispanic culture plays an important part in many segments of Spanish-speaking people's behavior and must be brought into consideration when making selections for gifted and talented programs and in teaching these youngsters. For example, in many Hispanic households children are taught not to be competitive and so the behavior of these children in school may be much different from what the school considers appropriate.

Finally, we must deal with another factor that tends to dampen the school success of lower-class black and Hispanic children, gifted or not. This is one of motivation. These children do not have as many adult models who would motivate them toward academic pursuits and high achievement. Their interests are more often developed in the streets of big cities where their adult models may not demonstrate behavior that would be reinforced by the cultural mainstream. The children are more apt to acquire interests and motivations that are more immediately gratifying than those offered by the schools, where frustration tolerance and delayed gratification are rewarded. For these three reasons, it is a fact that there are many gifted or talented minority children in the population whose potential may never be identified or developed and who may lack the essentials of even doing average work in school.

## Native Americans

*My culture, the Lakota culture, has an oral tradition, so I ordinarily reject writing. It is one of the white world's ways of destroying the cultures of non-European peoples, the imposing of an abstraction over the spoken relationship of a people.*

The above quotation was taken from a speech, "Fighting Words on the Future of the Earth" (48), by Russell Means, cofounder of the American Indian Movement. It illustrates two factors that we must be aware of in dealing with gifted and talented children among American Indians, or Native Americans, as they prefer to be called. First, it demonstrates how sensitive we must be to the culture of a people when we are identifying their children for special programming and how much attention we must give to the design and content of that program. Second it illustrates, as the Navaho teacher Anita Pfeiffer states, the pressure the Native American must endure in deciding to give up parts of the native culture in order to participate in the cultural mainstream. The feelings of alienation expressed by Native Americans are similar to the attitudes expressed by other minority groups in the United States. The passage quoted above illustrates the degree of resentment that the culturally different feel toward white middle-class America.

The cultural aspects we have referred to are good examples of how we should alter our manner of identifying and developing a gifted and talented program for the culturally different child. In the case of Native Americans, the children come from a culture with an oral tradition. This tradition should be used as part of our approach in identifying these children, and its skills should be incorporated into any program we present to Native American youngsters. Now, it is true that if these children are eventually to compete in the mainstream culture they will need to develop many of the abilities that culture values, but this does not mean they must abandon their own cultural heritage.

It appears that when Native Americans have accepted or learned something from the mainstream culture they often feel that they have rejected part of their own culture. This implies that their children may not be very motivated to learn "white man's ways," as education in our schools appears to them. We are dealing with many potentially talented youngsters with whom we will have great difficulty in working because they lack the desire to achieve by our standards. If we are sensitive to the values and feelings of other cultural groups we can work with them, instead of against them, to bring forth the potential of their children.

## The Asian Cultures

When we refer to Asian cultures we are talking about very diverse peoples. There has been considerable debate as to whether their attitude toward achievement is markedly different from that of the mainstream culture. Again there is the question of a language barrier. Yet this seems to be a secondary difficulty; other cultural aspects may be more of a factor.

Asians in this country have traditionally avoided standing out as a group. They do not like to bring attention to themselves. Even in their communications they may be indirect, soft-spoken, and talk only when they have something of significance to say. Many Asian children are at a disadvantage when compared with their outspoken middle-class counter-parts. Program development must take these facts into consideration.

One Asian girl, Marcy, was discovered to be gifted by sheer chance. She was so quiet in class that her teacher thought she didn't know the work. When the teacher could not get responses from her for a certain assignment in math, she asked one of the "brighter" students to sit and tutor Marcy. It turned out that Marcy knew more than her tutor and did not require help at all. What she did require was a soft-spoken approach and understanding.

Not all Asian children fit the picture we have just presented. Many of them are fully as competitive as the middle-class white youngster. We have observed Asian children in gifted and talented programs and not been aware that they were at a disadvantage.

## Identification

How does one recognize a gifted or talented minority child? It is most important to look at the whole child, no matter who the child is, but for minorities it is especially important. One thing that can be done is to redesign the Renzulli-Hartman checklist (given in Chapter 5) and use it for the able disadvantaged pupil. The list can be made to refer more directly to the culture from which the child comes, in particular placing less emphasis on book learning and more on learning from experience. The Los Angeles Unified School District in California is one place where this has been done; the descriptions it uses are a good example of how to assess the behaviors of the culturally different.

When screening either disadvantaged or culturally different students, educators must look for those sparks in their school work that distinguish them from the balance of the class. They must review intelligence results in a skeptical manner and pay particular attention to the variability of subtest results. Rather than looking at the total IQ score, they should examine the child's strengths and weaknesses on different parts of the test. The quality of the responses as well as creativity is most important in evaluating the responses. "Street smartness" should also be considered; it is not measured on any test but may be an indication of potential.

One example of such a gifted child was Jack, a black youngster who when tested received an IQ of 96. While this score is considered average for the general population, it was a good performance for this disadvantaged child. It is true that his score was far below the level of children typically taken into gifted and talented programs, but a conversation with this young man revealed that the score in no way reflected his potential. He was well spoken and street sharp and exhibited good thinking and analytic skills. He was able to give sound reasoning for his actions and was respected as a leader among his friends. He always seemed to be one step ahead of the authorities and unfortunately was headed in the wrong direction. He was not concerned with school, nor with developing his special talents, not even with sports. Like many other disadvantaged youths, he was interested ony in making a fast dollar and receiving immediate gratification. It would be nice if this story had a happy ending, if we could report that this boy and his talents had been "reclaimed." This was not the case, and the situation probably will be typical until educators take a more active interest in developing the skills of very young minority children.

If gifted and talented education is to be offered equally to various subgroups of children, we will have to develop a separate set of norms for each group. That this is a monumental task can be attested to by the years of work required to develop existing tests. In addition, critics have questioned the value of developing separate identification criteria. If every group has its own set of norms for identification and its own separate approach to learning skills, how can we ever come up with a unified whole? Ultimately, critics ask, shouldn't we try to get the different cultural groups to work together to develop children who have the capability to add to the quality of human life? The answer to these questions is that we must not sacrifice the positive qualities of any culture in the name of assimilation. Americans tend to believe that equality in education means that everyone must be the same—but diversity in society is what keeps it growing.

## The Handicapped Child

The best way to introduce a discussion of the handicapped gifted would be to give an example. Roy came from a very poor home and while this probably contributed heavily to his school problems, the school staff also identified a specific learning disability. Diagnostically, Roy's overall IQ was in the bright-normal range but his profile revealed significant variability on subtests. He had remarkable strengths in vocabulary, a general fund of information, and ability to abstract, all of which were considered to be either superior or very superior. The presence of these skills was unusual in a child who came from such a disadvantaged background and who was encountering such a large amount of academic frustration.

Roy was reading well below grade level although his math achievement was somewhat above expectation. His profile suggested that he was a gifted, learning-disabled child in need of special programming. The gifts and talents of many children like Roy may be hidden by a handicapping condition. In Roy's case, the classroom teacher had never attended to the erratic nature of his skills because she had been too worried about his inability to read. Still, during testing the learning disabilities specialist noted advanced language skills. In one instance, when he was asked to use the color blue in a task, Roy asked, "Do you want sky blue or violet blue?" For a seven-year-old child from a deprived background this was a noteworthy response. Roy has bloomed in special education. In addition, he has been placed in a class with other gifted children and his classroom teacher notes that his verbal skills have benefited from his exposure to these youngsters.

## The Physically Disabled

A handicapping condition may be a physical, an emotional, or a learning disability. A physical handicap can be a condition such as blindness, deafness, orthopedic disability, or severe neurological impairment. Children with such disabilities are often missed as being gifted or talented for a number of reasons.

First, staff and parents are so involved with the physical disability that they often miss certain talents the children have. Second, conventional diagnostic testing often is not sensitive to their intellectual talents because these measures often require the use of the physical attribute these children do not have.

A case in point is a hard-of-hearing youngster who was very weak in language areas on intelligence testing but did well on nonverbal areas. If it were not for this boy's physical condition, he would have definitely scored in the superior or very superior range. Because of his disability his true potential was not discovered until much later. Of course, he could not func-tion in a regular school setting without special education, but in a special program for the deaf he was taught ways of compensating for his disability.

## Two Case Studies

As we talk about the physically handicapped gifted child two other boys come to mind, both of whom have to cope with the disability of visual impairment.

Jodi is an alert, curious five-year-old who lost nearly all of his vision due to cancer as an infant. Today he has some vision in one eye but as he describes it, "All I can see is fuzzy light and dark." Jodi attended a regular nursery school program where he seemed to make a good adjustment. When he began kindergarten in the fall he traveled on the regular bus, much to his mother's trepidation. Jodi, however, did not seem overly distressed by the limitations his condition imposed. Within the first few months of school he learned rapidly how to get around the entire school layout, and could at times be seen running from place to place with his instructor.

Jodi wasn't fazed by the testing session either. Like many bright children he resisted the rote memory tasks, complaining that they were "boring," but he obtained an IQ of 124 on a regular Stanford-Binet, L-M. This is particularly remarkable because this test is not designed for the visually impaired. Yet with some modification in the testing procedure, Jodi had been able to perform in the superior range. Jodi's tactile skills (which involves the sense of touch) were remarkable. Even on a picture where someone traced the outline with Jodi's finger and left out some important feature, he was able to tell what had been omitted.

Jodi's ability to discriminate sounds was also acute. After meeting his special teacher only a few times Jodi commented, "I knew it was you, I could tell from your footsteps."

Socially Jodi gravitated to other children in his class whom the staff considered gifted. He seemed to form positive relationships with them and was accepted despite his obvious disability.

Even though it would not be considered a necessary skill for a blind child, Jodi taught himself to identify the letters of the alphabet and some numbers, by touch. It is hoped that with a

concerted staff effort Jodi will eventually be ready to participate in his district's gifted and talented program, which begins
in the middle elementary grades. Jodi evidences every indication of being not only a gifted child but far more able than
even his IQ test score would suggest. This is another instance
where testing supplies only a minimal estimate of that quality which we label intelligence.

This brings us to the question of selecting the hearing- or
vision-impaired student for a gifted and talented program. Chet
will exemplify the difficulties that are encountered when making this type of placement.

Chet was an albino youngster who had visual limitations
but could see well enough to read and get around. Like Jodi
he was alert, interested, and gave the impression of self-
confidence. Chet's group achievement scores were erratic
and his group IQ scores ranged from average to superior. This
type of variability in his group scores was not unexpected,
since group tests emphasize visual details that Chet would
have difficulty with.

It was Chet's "special" teacher who pushed his nomination
for the gifted and talented program. She stated that he often
surprised her with his abilities, and she thought he should be
given a chance to demonstrate how well he could perform.
Understandably the classroom teacher had a more difficult
time estimating Chet's potential. He definitely felt that Chet
had more ability than his classroom performance indicated.
On the Renzulli-Hartman checklist he rated Chet very highly
on learning and creativity characteristics and somewhat lower
on motivational and leadership factors.

The selection committee spent considerable time debating
Chet's candidacy. There was no question that he was a
gifted child—both the teacher's evaluation and the verbal
section of an individual IQ test suggested very high potential. The debate revolved around Chet's erratic achievement
and his ability to balance the demands of both the classroom and the special program. Another issue was whether
the program itself might need major adaptations to deal
with Chet's disability. Information from special services indicated that modifications would be minimal. It was finally
decided to go ahead and give Chet a chance to participate in
the program.

All the staff were pleasantly surprised that few difficulties
presented themselves during Chet's first year in the program.

He demonstrated original work in writing, and he insisted on doing many of the artistic tasks with the rest of the class, despite his disability. His cartoons showed a keen sense of humor and far more ability in this area than anyone had expected.

While Chet's placement has been a success, it is well to keep in mind that his visual disability was minor compared with Jodi's. One thing is certain: Chet's success has smoothed the way for other handicapped children to enter the gifted and talented program in his district. His performance has helped to dispel the fears and misperceptions the staff had had about dealing with the handicapped gifted child.

Major adjustments will have to be made in programs for the gifted and talented if they are to service disabled children with significant handicaps. Here is the place where the special education staff must work hand in hand with the gifted and talented program staff. Not only do visually and hearing-impaired students require curriculum adaptations but they need support in order to complete all their academic responsibilities.

The same problems that we have seen with the hearing and visually impaired occur with other physical disabilities. We often miss the true potential of these students because of the disability. It seems imperative that these children be offered special programs not only for their physical disabilities but also for their gifted and talented attributes. Sometimes this can be done in the mainstream of the regular school program, but oftentimes it cannot. Parents of these children need special counseling to help them understand their child and to make sure they do not let the physical disability become a handicap in the true sense of the word and an excuse for not producing academically.

## The Learning Disabled

The second category of the gifted handicapped are those children with a learning disability. What is a learning disability? This is an area in education on which it is difficult to get any two professionals to agree. The reason for the many disagreements is that educators try to fit this concept into a nice neat box when the dynamics of it make such a task impossible. A learning disability is too complex a situation to attribute to one or two causes, as many people try to do. It is not a germ that a child can catch while walking down the street. It is a multifactored situation that calls for examining the whole child in order to make the corrections the youngster needs to learn.

Evidence that a child has a learning disability, in its simplest terms, appears in a situation in which a child is not working up to his or her potential. The reasons for the discrepancy between potential and actual performance usually do not include, as the *primary* cause, physical handicaps such as those already mentioned, emotional disturbances, and disadvantaged environments. They do include conditions such as minimal neurological impairment, perceptual difficulties, and aphasia. This, however, is not enough. Learning disabilities are not caused by any single factor unless it is a severe condition. Learning disabilities are the result of many factors, including, besides those mentioned, predisposition to learning (learning style), interaction with personality factors, and—most important—attention and concentration. When we say "multifactored," we mean that a single weakness in a child is not usually enough to create a learning disability.

Evelyn is a typical example of a gifted learning-disabled child. Her IQ was 133 but her reading comprehension level was two years behind grade expectation. Evelyn appeared to be a socially and emotionally intact youngster who had difficulties in short-term memory areas. Interestingly, although she had an IQ in the very superior range, Evelyn's thinking style was rigid. She could not shift her thoughts from one subject to the next. Her strengths were in convergent thinking skills. She could feed back what she was taught, but she could not generalize or make inferences from the information she learned. When one looked at Evelyn's learning style, it was apparent that her overconforming behavior was reflective of overcontrolling and strict parents. Evelyn's parents raised her to be a "good" girl in the extreme, to conform to the rules at hand, to obey authority.

Although there is nothing inherently wrong in the values her parents instilled, this type of attitude in child rearing can aggravate learning problems when carried to the extreme. The result was an intelligent and socially mature youngster who could not think.

The example of Curt will demonstrate how diverse the group of gifted learning-disabled children actually is. Curt, at age eight, was referred to a psychologist by his parents because he was not doing well in reading and they believed he could do better. Curt was the youngest of three children; his older brother had been involved in the school's gifted and talented program. Unlike Evelyn's parents, Curt's family was supportive and nonpressuring. While they were interested in education, they realized that all their children were different and might not achieve on the same level. If Curt was haunted by the specter of his talented sibling it was through his own doing. Still, Curt's parents felt he was too bright to be doing barely grade-level work in reading. The psychological evaluation justified their concern.

Curt's teacher described him as a bright child who was well spoken and used a sophisticated vocabulary. She stated that Curt performed as well as he did in reading and spelling only because of a conscious effort. She related that he became extremely upset under pressure and that it was apparent he did not want to fail in any way. Curt said that failure "embarrassed" him. When he faced testing in his "weak" subjects he would begin to cry and carry on. It was these emotional aspects of the situation that convinced his parents that they were correct in their belief that there was something wrong with his reading and that something should be done about it.

During evaluation Curt was a friendly, cooperative boy who verbalized easily. He was alert and seemed interested in the tasks, and he exhibited no signs of anxiety.

Curt's style told a lot about his problems in reading and spelling. He encountered difficulty in any area where symbols (denotative signs) were a chief element. He seemed to have trouble holding purely symbolic material in his memory, especially when it was read to him. He had to resort to his fingers for math computations. To compensate for this problem Curt would talk continually to himself during symbolic tasks to aid his analysis and memory.

While Curt's individual IQ scores showed a performance in the very superior range (IQ 139), his achievement tests indicated a performance barely close to grade level in most areas of reading. Only reading comprehension and math achievement were close to expectation.

Following evaluation, Curt received the additional services he needed. His special teacher is helping him work toward a better than grade-level achievement in reading, which would be more in keeping with his ability, and is preparing him for a chance to participate in his school's gifted and talented program. As his confidence builds, Curt is no longer wary of testing or of reading itself.

## Children with Emotional Problems

The child with an emotional handicap or the emotionally disturbed child is one we all think we know about until we ask ourselves what emotional disturbance is. First of all, a child with emotional problems is one whose behavior is deviant from that of other children. This deviant behavior is not caused by physiological deficits but is the result of learning from the environment. Thus a child with emotional problems cannot cope with his or her world, or responds to this world in a deviant way as a result of misdirected learning. For example, such a child may have developed feelings of inadequacy because parents have been highly critical; these feeling may cause the child to withdraw in social situations and to hesitate to try in school.

The underachieving child is an example of one form of emotional problem among the gifted. Not all gifted children with emotional problems show deviance in achievement. Many of them achieve as would be expected in school but show deficits in other areas. In a sense, though, they are all exhibiting underachievement in some area of life. Most would be considered unhappy and maladjusted.

All emotionally disturbed people fit into one of the following groups. Either they are hurting others by their behavior, or, they are hurting themselves by their behavior, or they are doing both. Most emotionally disturbed individuals do both most of the time.

This behavior may be exhibited to varying degrees. When we talk about hurting others or oneself we may not be talking about severe situations. The person's problem may be limited to self-embarrassment or being verbally hostile to another— certainly less extreme than inflicting physical harm on oneself by constantly getting into accidents.

One such gifted emotionally disturbed young man related how he constantly had ups and downs throughout his life, which were the result of his own doing. Every success that he earned for himself he would find some way to destroy. This young man was a highly gifted individual who had few difficulties in his school years. College and graduate work in business were also fairly successful, but he never really was as successful as he was capable of being, because of the hostility he turned toward himself whenever he was doing well. This was really an expression of hostility that he felt toward his parents; in addition, he had incorporated his parents' desires to hurt him, which they had unconsciously suggested to him as a youngster.

There are some gifted children whose social and emotional problems can be alleviated somewhat by appropriate programming. One such girl, a first grader named Rachel, was very aggressive toward other children and baffled teachers with her good excuses for why she could not get along with others. Rachel was in a regular school program where she found the work easy and boring. A shift to the district's gifted program helped in this regard and her aggression toward her classmates diminished. Psychotherapy was still needed to help Rachel with her social and emotional problems, but the school pressures were certainly lessened by the move.

With most gifted or talented children with emotional difficulties, psychotherapy does not seem to be enough. It is imperative that environmental factors such as school programs be altered. This may call for the school to provide counseling services or academic changes for more success or chances for better peer interactions with children who demonstrate appropriate and productive behaviors. In addition, the parents' participation in the psychotherapy and the school changes is very important. Without parental support, any child's chances for progress are considerably reduced.

## Summing Up

Women, the handicapped, the disadvantaged, and the culturally different gifted and talented are groups that are often forgotten. Their giftedness is easy to overlook; but even if it is recognized, these select groups within a select group require even more time and effort on the part of the school than do the usual gifted or talented. It is gratifying, however, that these groups have not been forgotten by the experts in education. In a world troubled by overpopulation and a devaluing of the individual, these groups have been remembered because we are in need of the skills of all our citizens. Our world is plagued with economic shortages and is flirting with disaster, and the most valuable resource we have is the talent of our youth. To leave out any potentially gifted child is a tragedy not only to the individual but to the world.

# 8
# Where Do We Go From Here?

W e have planned the foregoing sections of this book to serve as a frame of reference for the last two chapters. In the present chapter we will focus on how to deal with testing and formal education; in the final one we will discuss home stimulation, social skills, and parent organizations. The information will be most useful if you remember that we are discussing the gifted and talented in general. There are ex-. ceptions to every rule, and your child may very well be the exception. Our suggestions should be considered additional information, to be used in concert with advice from the professionals who know your child personally.

## Working with or against the System

Let us begin with the statement that you should not assume you must take an adversary role when dealing with the school system. Attitudes toward gifted and talented education vary considerably, and can even take diametrically opposed positions in neighboring school districts. Do not be too quick to place blame!

You should realize that the feelings and inclinations of your local school staff may be severely limited by district policy. For example, a principal may clearly see that your child needs acceleration, but if central administration has decreed a "no grade skipping" regulation, the principal will be wary of creating a confrontation. He or she may promote the child on the sly, swearing all to secrecy (and hoping not to be found out by upper administration until much later), may simply refuse to make the move, or may fob you off on a superior. It helps here to find out the philosophy and internal structure of the district. Sometimes parents move to a certain school district because they have "heard" that the gifted and talented program there is very good; later they are disappointed in the program's quality, and feel they have been misled. Their perceptions may not be exactly accurate. The program may in fact be much better than anything offered in the vicinity, even though it does not compare favorably with model programs around the country. Part of the parents' misconception was that they heard only what they wanted to hear and did not objectively assess the district's offerings before they moved in. Therefore, their disappointment was largely a result of unrealistic expectations.

Let us discuss a case where this type of disenchantment did not occur. Lilly's family was relocating from one section of the country to another. In her previous school, Lilly had been accelerated a grade. Now her parents had to decide whether she should participate in the new school's gifted and talented program. They were not quite sure whether she was truly gifted, and if so, to what degree or in what ways. They were concerned as well whether their child should be placed in the program with her age peers, or with the children at her grade level who had already participated in the program for a year. They believed that placement was a major issue both because Lilly was not yet eight years old and because of the degree of isolation caused by a move of many hundreds of miles. These parents dealt with the issues in two ways.

Initially they had Lilly's skills assessed to determine her level of functioning in a variety of academic areas. They obtained an estimation of her strengths, weaknesses, and personality style. Simultaneously, they explored the makeup of the new program, to decide whether its emphasis fit in with Lilly's profile. They were thus able to determine realistically both what they could expect from Lilly and what the school system could provide. They were confident in enrolling their daughter in the special program because they were thoroughly informed and had developed realistic expectations.

## Two Children

There are as few absolutes in education as there are in life in general. This applics both to how much parents cooperate with the school and how schools deal with parents. Let's examine two different situations, one in which the school and parents were able to work together and another in which they could not. The youngsters in each case were just entering kindergarten.

During orientation, Stephen's father told the principal and kindergarten teacher that his son was already reading. Stephen, who was acting like a typical five-year-old, did not initially impress the staff as exceptional. However, his teacher, a perceptive person, realized that intellectual skills and behavior do not necessarily go hand in hand. She adopted a wait-and-see attitude. Within two weeks of the beginning of school, Stephen's reading ability was apparent, and the teacher requested an individual reading evaluation. Results indicated that Stephen's reading ranged between fifth- and sixth-grade levels; his comprehension was almost as good as his analysis of words and vocabulary. While the reading specialist was selecting appropriate material for Stephen to work with, the school psychologist examined his other skills. Some fine motor (such as drawing) lags were shown. Together, the staff planned a program for Stephen and another child who was also reading. Each day some time was set aside for both children to develop their reading as well as a mutual interest in science. Attention was given to improving Stephen's motor ability. Conferences were held with his parents both to keep them informed of their son's progress and to suggest things for them to do with him at home. Together, parents and staff forged a positive working relationship before Stephen entered first grade.

Kathy's experience was not as fortunate. Kathy was adopted from a foreign country. Her parents were quite worried that she might be handicapped because she came from a deprived environment. They had never considered that she might be gifted and they were simply relieved that she was developing "normally." It was not until they began to have other children that they realized that Kathy was a very quick learner. Still, they did not start to think of her as gifted until she began to read and do simple arithmetic on her own. By the time Kathy entered kindergarten, her reading ability was only a shade less dramatic than Stephen's. But math was her most remarkable skill. Kathy had figured out simple addition and subtraction on her own and was plaguing her mother to teach her double-digit addition and subtraction. She was also experimenting with multiplication and fractions. Kathy's parents had high hopes for her when she entered school.

For several weeks all was peaceful. Kathy spoke little about her class, but her parents thought nothing of this. Imagine their shock and horror when they were called to school because Kathy was described as a terrible behavior problem.

Both Kathy and her teacher saw her behavior the same way. Kathy refused to fit in. The school curriculum called for her to cut and paste and do whatever else her classmates were doing. Kathy insisted that she also wanted to read and do math. The situation reached a total impasse. Neither side would budge. In desperation, Kathy's parents placed her in therapy. While her behavior improved, she was very unhappy. Her parents tried to negotiate some individualized attention for first grade, without any success. The final result was that Kathy was sent to a private school where she was accelerated a grade and socially, fit in well with children a year older than she. While Kathy's story ended happily enough, she and her parents were left with a bitter taste from dealing with the system.

These two examples suggest that an individual's experience with the schools is as likely to be good as it is to be negative. In order to deal most effectively with your child's educational experience, it is best to approach planning in the structured manner used by Lilly's parents.

# Testing

Let us now take a step-by-step journey from preschool through high school graduation. A logical place to begin is with the area of testing.

## How Young to Test

Unless your child is *very* remarkable, it is not advisable to have him or her tested prior to the third birthday. How unusual is a very remarkable child? If your under-three-year-old is reading books with very few pictures, doing simple arithmetic, playing a musical instrument, acquiring another language through a crack-of-dawn TV show (like "Sunrise Semester") or showing other similar behavior, then you might consider early assessment. We would still prefer to wait until just a little later to do formal testing. It is not so much the behavior but the age of the child exhibiting the behavior that is remarkable. Preschool children have short attention spans. Even gifted preschoolers who demonstrate longer attention spans than their peers will have a hard time sitting though an assessment. When children are under three, they will also be more reluctant to leave their parents and stay for a relatively long period of time with a stranger. It is preferable for them to have been exposed to a structured situation such as nursery school before the evaluation is done. Children with some experience in following directions and producing work on demand will be more ready to adapt to the rigors of testing.

Despite what many educators would like us to believe, there is no reason not to have a four- or five-year-old tested if you believe the child is gifted. The case is often made that it is impossible accurately to test preschool gifted children. That is nonsense. No one questions the need for early assessment of the handicapped or the accuracy of such evaluations. Gifted children stand out from their peers as much as handicapped children. It is therefore logical to assume that we can provide preschool gifted children with a fairly accurate evaluation. While test results on IQ measures have been shown to be slightly less reliable under the age of seven, the difference is not great enough to cause any concern. If you are interested in the child's style and relative strengths and weaknesses, it will not matter if the IQ numbers vary somewhat from estimate to estimate. Remember that for intelligence testing to be useful, undue emphasis should not be put on the IQ number itself.

Our own preference is for individual assessment to take place sometime before second grade. Many of the gifted children who stop performing at high and unusual levels do so by the time they are in second grade. If our goal is to identify as many gifted children as possible, we should start looking for them at the kindergarten level, before they are turned off by school.

## Where Should I Have My Child Tested?

There are various answers to this question. If the child is a preschooler, you should seek psychological and educational

assessment either from some center that specializes in working with the gifted and talented (such as a university affili-
ated with gifted programs) or from a private specialist in the
field. If the child is of school age, then you may want the
school to test your child. You are entitled to free assessment
just as if your child were handicapped. However, bear in
mind that in states without laws pertaining to gifted education, you will probably have to wait a long time for an evaluation. Because your child's testing will probably not be seen
as a serious problem, you may find yourself at the bottom of
a long waiting list. Under such circumstances you may decide to get the testing done elsewhere. Children whose talent
is in art or music will generally have to be evaluated outside
the schools if you expect assessment prior to the fourth
grade.

## Who Should Test My Child?

As in any other field, credentials are important. In your regular school, psychologists, reading specialists, and other professionals must all meet specific certification requirements.
Testing administered by these individuals should be fairly accurate. How much experience they have with the gifted and
talented is another issue; it can vary from professional to professional. If you think that experience is an issue, inquire
about the tester's background.

Contrary to what you may think, you must actually be *more*
careful in selecting an outside professional than in having
someone in the school do the testing. First, ask to see credentials. Psychologists should be licensed in those states that require a license. Teachers should have certification in reading if
they claim to be reading specialists. Experts in areas like music
or art should likewise have credentials to show you. Beware of
charlatans who claim to be experts and simply hope clients
won't question their expertise. Try to select a psychologist
who works with children if you can't find one experienced in
gifted education. Many psychologists in private practice are
concerned with the adjustment problems of adults and are un-
used to working with or evaluating the learning styles of children. Many private practitioners are solely therapists and do
not do assessment at all. If there is a local association for the
gifted and talented you can consult it for a qualified person.
Another source of referral would be your local psychological

association. Regardless of whom you choose, you need to make the selection as an informed consumer.

## What If My Child Is Referred as a Problem?

If your child is not performing in the classroom, or is exhibiting disruptive behavior, you may be asked to have him or her evaluated by the school staff. Should you do this? In our opinion there is no real reason to refuse. School evaluation is a service you are already paying for with your tax dollars. You can always seek a second opinion from an outside professional should the need arise. Records are considered restricted material and *cannot* be released without your permission. Neither will the record of past problems always follow the child, especially when there is no further recurrence of the problem. Use school assessment for what it is—one sampling of behavior and academic and intellectual functioning. Many times in-house testing has located gifted and talented children who might otherwise have been overlooked. Ralph is one such case.

Ralph was referred to a psychologist because he could not get along with his peers. Ralph's father also found it difficult to relate to his son. The evaluation showed a boy functioning well above grade level in achievement with a full IQ of 132. The classroom teacher was so focused on Ralph's behavior that she had overlooked the boy's achievement, and would never have nominated him for a gifted and talented program. Ralph was accepted into the program, but not without some trepidation on the part of the staff. He made a surprisingly good adjustment to the program, however, even though his peer interactions were still below average. The problem between Ralph and his father also continued to exist, but observers noted that he was not the same obnoxious little boy that he had been. Without the school's evaluation, Ralph might never have been nominated and allowed to participate in the gifted and talented program.

## What Should an Evaluation Include?

If your child is being evaluated in or out of school, whether for a problem, to enter a gifted and talented program, or just to help you understand him or her better, you should try to obtain the most comprehensive evaluation available. This means that besides an individual IQ test you should expect some assessment of achievement, fine motor skills, creativity, and personality. Your child is a whole person and should be assessed as such. (This type of total assessment is more difficult with very young children, because of more limited test options and the children's shorter attention span.) Wherever possible, ask for some description of the child's learning style, because good planning must be based on a breakdown of the tested skills.

## What about Reports?

You are entitled to a copy (at minimal cost) of any reports that are in your child's school folder. It is good practice to retain copies of the evaluation report for your own records, especially in case you move. While records can be forwarded, it is always safer to have a copy of your own. It can provide the new school with the information at the time you are registering, so that they can begin immediately to make an appropriate placement for your child. This will save you and your child the aggravation of having to have another evaluation. However, if the report is more than two years old, the school may request permission to do a current assessment of the child's skills.

Reports from an outside professional need to be managed in much the same manner. Try to obtain two or three copies of the report, so that you can keep one and will be able to give one to the school. Another option is to sign a release that allows the examiner to mail a copy of the findings directly to the school. Whichever method you choose, be sure you understand the report as fully as you can. It is impossible to discuss planning intelligently if you do not comprehend what needs to be done for your child.

# Picking the Proper Program

## Choosing a Preschool

The initial step in choosing a preschool is to be realistic about your child and your family situation. First you must consider your child's social maturity. No matter how bright children are, if they are socially immature, they are not ready for a program with a heavy academic orientation. Next consider the age of the child. Younger preschoolers are generally not suited to an all-day, five-day-a-week program. Better to start a three-year-old with half days and progress at the age of four to a more extensive commitment.

What can you afford to spend, and how will the child get to the school? These are two issues you must face. No matter how good the school, it is not worth the child's spending half the day on a bus going to class and home again. Determine if the cost of the program is justified. Are the facilities in good repair, materials new and/or well cared for, and the professional staff well trained? What is the school's educational philosophy with respect to gifted and talented children? Is the school prepared to provide advanced academic skills if the child is ready for them? Be sure to visit the program, preferably more than once. Try to bring your child to see the school. You can both be more objective about the situation if you assess it together. Don't be afraid to ask questions—how are the children disciplined? does the school offer a day that the child can "try out" the program? Most of all, don't be afraid to switch programs in midstream if you find that all is not well. Nothing is gained by suffering through an inappropriate placement.

## What about Kindergarten?

Many parents ask whether they should switch their children from a private preschool to a public one when it is time for kindergarten. Is it better to wait until first grade to shift placement? Again a number of factors are involved. Visit your local school and find out what type of kindergarten program it offers. If the program is designed mainly to foster social skill development *and* your child is coming from an academically oriented preschool, it is probably preferable to wait to make the switch in schools. If your child is in an all-day class and the kindergarten program is a half-day session, you may also opt to maintain a private preschool placement. Don't forget the social factors, however. Bear in mind that all the child's friends may be going to the public kindergarten. You should consider his or her reaction to that social reality. The best advice is to use common sense and balance your child's academic and social requirements. Decide what you need and which placement offers the most for your purposes.

## Early Admission Revisited

Should you seek early admission to kindergarten or first grade? By and large, for the mature child, early admission is quite beneficial. If you are thinking about this option, the initial move is to find out the school's policies. In some cases the school will grant early admission to first grade if the child has attended a private kindergarten.

Early admission to kindergarten usually involves the child's participating in the school's kindergarten screening (and doing as well as the older children taking these tests) or having an individual evaluation by an outside professional. In either instance the goal is to make sure that the child is emotionally and academically ready for kindergarten. The child who has not attended a preschool program may be at a decided disadvantage during such a screening. Again, be honest with yourself as to whether early admission is the best course for your child. He or she may do as well with another year of preschool, if the overall social and academic areas are not exceptionally advanced.

## At What Grade Do Most Special Programs Start?

Gifted and talented programs most frequently begin at the third grade, and go to the sixth grade. Programs for younger children are infrequent, because of the biases of schools. Administrators do not want to say too early that a child is gifted, for fear of making a mistake in identification. While it is true that there is some variance in evaluation techniques, it is not great enough to justify not identifying and servicing children. Administrators should recall that they have no such qualms about identifying the young handicapped. A second bias on the part of most school staff and many parents is their belief that very young children either cannot think well enough or are too socially or physically immature to participate in special programs. This is a myth. While it may be better not to bus very young children hither and yon for special classes, there is no reason that individualized programming can't be done in the regular school. This is the perfect situation for clustering and in-house resource room classes. Much less time will need to be devoted to unlearning poor work habits if good planning begins in the lower grades. If we are to move toward implementing Renzulli's Level III programming (see Chapter 5), we must begin our overall efforts at an early age.

## What about Programs at the Secondary Level?

If it can be said that gifted and talented programs in elementary schools emphasize grades three through six, then secondary schools put most of their emphasis on honors (accelerated) tracks and advanced placement courses. In some cases secondary level students are able to take courses at local universities or work with a faculty member as a mentor in an area of interest. Overall, there has been less change for the gifted and talented at the secondary school level than at the elementary level. This situation probably will not continue for long because of the number of elementary level programs that are cropping up around the country. One group of secondary school teachers did some volunteer work in an elementary gifted and talented program; they came to realize that, given the activities the children were doing as well as the rapid progression of their skills, modifications were going to be needed in the secondary honors curriculum. In the near future many secondary schools will have to face these facts. You cannot expect to provide the same old secondary curriculum to students who have spent up to six years in special programming, and who may now be capable of running experiments or doing other advanced work usually undertaken by graduate students.

## To Accelerate or Not to Accelerate

While there is considerable talk about enrichment, professionals are generally in agreement that at a certain point, enrichment must stop and content acceleration take over. Thus, most gifted and talented children involved in special programs will be exposed to this type of acceleration as a matter of course. The type of acceleration parents are more concerned about, however, is grade skipping.

Like early admission, grade skipping must be handled with common sense. Let us examine the case of Mary. Mary was a mature first grader in a private school. The classes in the school were very large (close to 40 children in each one) and any extra enrichment had to be provided by parent volunteers. Mary had begun to complain to her parents that she was bored, but unfortunately her teacher had no time or resources to develop individualized instruction. The result was that the school began to consider acceleration as a partial solution. Mary took a series of tests to assess her skills. Math performance on two measures—the Wide Range Achievement Test and the Peabody Individual Achievement Test (both individual tests)—estimated Mary's skills to be at a beginning fourth-grade level. Mary took the Green level of the Stanford Diagnostic Reading Test, which compared her performance to a third-grade scale; children in her grade would typically take a much easier version of this test. Her performance on the Stanford was also remarkable, with scores ranging from mid-second grade to early sixth-grade levels. Mary's stanines in reading were thus considered average or better for a child in the third grade. Intelligence test analysis showed an unusually even profile of skills that balanced at a 140 IQ. Examination of the results suggested that Mary exhibited real talent in math.

The school began to let Mary spend some time each day with a second-grade class to familiarize her with both the children and the work expected. The procedure worked very well, and Mary soon acted as if she had always been part of the class. The other children accepted her presence with only a minimal adjustment period. At the end of first grade Mary went on to third grade with this class, and at last report was doing very well.

This was not the case for Patti, who was also accelerated, but in a different school. Patti's kindergarten performance on achievement and intelligence tests was only slightly less remarkable than Mary's. However, Patti was an immature child who was not ready for the structure of a first-grade class. Nevertheless, Patti's parents were insistent that her placement be changed, and at last the school gave in and moved her from kindergarten to first grade. She was placed with some gifted first graders, both to allow the teacher to plan more accurately and in hopes that the other children's good work habits and mature peer interactions would be a good influence on her. The plan did not work out well. Four years later Patti is barely keeping up academically, not because of a lack of skills, but because she is still immature. She would have been better off spending the year in kindergarten rather than going on to first grade and a lackluster school career. If she had been tried part-time in first grade (as Mary was in second) her lack of readiness would have been more noticeable to her parents and the class switch avoided.

For the exceptionally gifted or talented child, content accel-eration may become as serious an issue as grade skipping. Laura was very similar to Mary when she was in second grade. She was markedly balanced in overall skills, but exhibited highly precocious math ability. In math her talent far ex-ceeded Mary's, and she was beginning geometry during the second grade. The elementary school gave her considerable enrichment in math but stopped short of letting her fully pursue secondary topics. In frustration Laura began getting texts from her local library, and pushed her mother to order math materials through the mail. The school believed that Laura was not really ready for secondary math, and thought she might be hurt by too early exposure to such advanced topics. By chance, Laura's family moved to another school district. Here she was allowed to follow her math interests. The teacher went to great lengths to acquire appropriate texts. Rather than suffering any ill effects, Laura was happier than she had been in a long time. Her parents are happy about the curriculum change as well. Unlike Patti's family, they had given serious thought to their decision, even writing to Dr. Julian Stanley's Study of Mathematically Precocious Youth (SMPY) project at Johns Hopkins University for advice.

Acceleration can be a beneficial tool when properly used. If you are thinking about acceleration, get a complete evalua-tion of your child. Consider how the move will affect the other children in your family. In one instance, parents refused to have their daughter double skipped because it would have placed her in the same grade with her more average older brother. They felt that the change would have been difficult enough in itself, without arousing the animosity of the child's sibling. If you have strong doubts about making such a move, get a second opinion to help in making a better decision.

## What about Private Schools?

Some parents believe that placing the child in private school will be the solution to their problems. They feel that because their fee payment is visible, and not hidden as it is in public school taxes, they will have more control over what the child is taught. They also feel that because of smaller classes the child will receive more individualized attention. Depending on the situation at the particular school, these beliefs may or may not materialize. Many private schools operate on a shoestring budget, and may in fact have less to offer than the local public school. They may not have the funds for laboratories or computers or an extensive library. They may not offer instrumental music or an extensive sports program. They are no more likely than any other school to have staff that is experienced in dealing with gifted and talented students. Many private schools, especially parochial ones, are beset with large classes that are not conducive to individualized instruction. When considering a private school, either at the elementary or the secondary level, evaluate it as you would a preschool. Check credentials, staff-to-pupil ratio, materials, educational orientation, and the type of children that attend. Many private schools cater to children who have behavior problems and are not able to succeed in the public school system. If the school you are looking into seems to have too many pupils with behavior or learning problems, it may not be the place for your child. Make sure the school is accredited by your state, and visit the facility several times. By and large, private schools are quite expensive, and you should be sure you are getting your money's worth.

There is no doubt that a good prep school may help to ready an able learner for admission to a good college. Check the school's record of placing children in the colleges you may be interested in having your child attend. Be wary of a special school for the gifted. Find out how long it has been in operation and what its reputation is before paying your fees. While it is true that interest in the gifted and talented has revived only recently, that does not justify a school that changes its brochure to attract more students. In an education field now experiencing the "bandwagon" phenomenon, you need to be more wary than ever of a school's claim to being expert in the instruction of the gifted and talented.

## What about Specialized
## Secondary Schools?

Many localities, in particular large cities, offer a variety of specialized schools for the gifted and the talented, such as the Bronx High School of Science in New York City. Again, you need to have a clear picture of your child's skills before making any decisions. Probably one of the hardest choices to make for many gifted children is whether to apply to such a specialized school. A large number of gifted and talented children actually have too many options open to them. Unless your child has one skill that stands out markedly from the others, you may be better off tryng for a well-rounded program. If your child has an exceptional talent in an area, such as math, dance, or music, you will have been aware of the talent long before the decision of whether to choose a specialized secondary school. This is a matter that is best handled by long-range planning. In any case, children who have an exceptional talent are frequently working with a mentor, either privately or through the school. It is best to ask that person, who is after all an expert in the particular field, about the advisability of a specialized school.

## Will a Gifted and Talented Program Be Detrimental to My Child?

Many, if not most, gifted and talented children are already aware that they are different. Their peers are also aware of this difference. In fact, peer awareness is so great that one method of identifying exceptional children is to ask their classmates to list their names. Thus, the mere fact of entering a gifted and talented program will not necessarily accentuate the difference further. When the gifted and talented program is handled like any other special program in the school district, there should be no difficulty with participation. It is only when too much ballyhoo takes place that problems begin. A large sign at the entrance of the school loudly proclaiming "this way to the gifted and talented classes" will certainly alienate children and staff alike. If the school suggests that the needs of the gifted are being catered to while others will have to get by as best they can, the program will alienate children and staff alike.

There can also be problems if you and your child do not deal with the situation properly. While you certainly have every right to be pleased that your child is participating in a gifted and talented program, try to temper the demonstration of your feelings. Do not allow your child to make too much of the class, because no one likes to listen to a braggart. Gifted and talented children must adopt the role of the graceful winner; they must understand that superior ability carries responsibility with it—part of which is empathy for the feelings of others. Most gifted and talented children will perceive this reality early in their school careers. If a child does not learn social awareness skills through observation and modeling, it is the parents' responsibility to educate him or her in the area.

Most gifted and talented children should be able to balance regular classroom demands and special program requirements. If your child cannot do this, then it is time to reconsider the placement. Most writers have suggested that gifted children finish their work with ease, and waste large amounts of time in the regular classroom. The child who is struggling under the additional work load may be disorganized or improperly placed in the program. Your child's complaint is a signal to consult all the staff about the true state of affairs. It may be that this is the first time he or she has had to work, and the child does not want to put in as much effort as is needed. Or it may be that there are too many busywork assignments to complete. It is possible that the child is afraid to ask someone for the work that is missed. The final line, however, may be that the special program is not suited to the needs of your child. If so, you should remove him or her from the class.

## Should I Consider Extracurricular Classes?

Whether you want to sign your child up for swimming, dance, music, or other types of lessons, be as careful when you do this as you are when selecting a regular school placement. Staff credentials are especially important when classes are extracurricular. Teachers of areas such as dance and music need to be more interested in what the children—especially the youngest children—learn in the course of the year than they are in the end of the year performances. Sports activities should be aimed at having fun while developing skills, and should avoid overemphasis on being first or winning. Remember that, first and foremost, your child *is* just a child. Don't overbook your youngster's time. Gifted and talented children tend to take on many projects on their own. If you fill their every free moment, they will have no opportunity for the incubation so crucial to creativity. On the other hand, do not be afraid to experiment. Participation in swimming for infants (sometimes as young as three or four months old) and early training on a musical instrument for toddlers are opportunities to learn self-discipline and independence. Older children and adolescents may be intrigued by advanced courses offered by local universities, museums, and other community groups. In some cases children may be in for a surprise when the curriculum is very challenging or they find that others are equally gifted. To satisfy the need for companionship and to learn humility, gifted and talented children need to face the reality that they are not unique in their talents.

# What Is an IEP?

The concept of the individual education plan (IEP) was born in special education and is now evolving into part of planning for the gifted and talented. Teachers who have had experience with IEPs in special education cringe at the mere mention of such individualized planning for the gifted. This is not necessary. Prescriptions for gifted and talented children do not necessarily require the exactness of specified content provided to handicapped or deprived individuals. After all, educators realize in most instances that they are looking at relative strengths and weaknesses in learning style as opposed to the actual deficits of the handicapped. Of course, when the child is handicapped or culturally different as well as gifted, the IEP will take on more complexity.

A second reason that IEPs for the gifted and talented are less specified in content is that these children are good learners of abstract concepts; they generally do not need a step-by-step breakdown of each task. In fact, they frequently resent the type of oversimplified, concrete instruction that typifies instruction for the handicapped. This does not mean that IEPs for the gifted should be superficial.

## How Good IEPs Are Developed

Donald Treffinger of the State University College at Buffalo, New York, has very effectively described how good IEPs for the gifted and talented ate characterized (30). He lists five areas around which to organize planning: (1) individualized basics; (2) appropriate enrichment; (3) effective acceleration; (4) development of independence and self-direction; and (5) values and personal development. The first step in implementing Treffinger's system is an assessment of the student's *current level of performance or functioning.*

### Current Functioning Level

To produce a quality academic plan for the child, a teacher must have estimates of the child's educational development. Whether the program is for the academically gifted or for the artistically talented, it is next to impossible to service the child properly without such a precise estimate of skills. This is why we have stressed the need for individual assessment. Group measures, because of both limited content and inaccurate estimates, do not provide a realistic picture of the child. Similar distortion is the product of using only full IQ numbers. This is the time for skill analysis in the manner of Guilford, for appropriate achievement testing or other professional assessment of the skill areas. Parents and educators must have an accurate picture of the student, have staff appropriately trained in the relevant analysis technique, and insist on adequate planning time. As an illustration, let us look at two boys, Robert and Chuck. Both of these children were seven and one-half years old when they entered a gifted program.

From first grade on, both boys showed reading and math performance on group achievement tests that was rated solidly ninth stanine. Group IQ scores on the Otis Lennon Mental Ability Test placed Robert's IQ at 135 and Chuck's at 126. Subsequent individual testing revealed both boys functioning overall at an IQ of 147. These identical scores are deceptive, however. Robert's score reflected more strength in math and nonlanguage areas, while Chuck's performance was typified by slightly stronger verbal skills. Both boys were functioning in math slightly lower than might have been expected for children of their overall ability. Again the reasons for this similar math level were entirely different in each child. Robert seemed merely to need exposure to basic skill areas in order to improve his performance. Chuck, on the other hand, exhibited difficulty in attending to detail, sequence, and general problem-solving skills.

A good IEP for each of these boys would need to address itself to these and other patterns in their profiles. For instance, Robert would probably be expected to make more rapid progress in improving his math skills than would Chuck, whose needs are more complex. None of this insight concerning the children's skills would have been obtained from a group score. Nor would it have been possible to decide what areas were especially strong and could be cultivated through enrichment.

Once a skill profile is obtained, long- and short-term goals can be set. The short-term goals will probably be centered on skill development (Treffinger's individualized basics) and enrichment, while long-term goals will reflect effective acceleration, independence, and personal development.

## The Next Step

At the time skills are assessed, it can be determined whether any related service is needed, and what personnel, other than the teacher of the gifted program, will be needed to work with the child. Such personnel might include a secondary school teacher, an older student mentor, or someone volunteering from the community. In addition, both the teacher's and the student's preferred style of learning should be analyzed. Does the child like to work alone, with a small group, or with many others; prefer projects, or peer teaching, or independent study? What does the teacher prefer? Once these preferences have been determined, they can then be melded with the program goals.

Effective planning should begin with the concept that curriculum development evolves from the needs of the students and not the other way around. Student grouping must be a result of their needs and not of convenience; it should be based on their academic skill profiles, and student and teacher personality styles. Individualized planning does *not* mean isolation of the student; the IEP is a team effort. The teachers, psychologist, parents, student, and administrator are all part of the team. For planning to be effective, the IEP must be a working tool, not somebody's grandiose creation. Good records must be kept so that the student's progress can be monitored and the curriculum revised as needed.

The child is not a static or unchanging organism. Good IEPs and good programs are responsive to change. Good planning is also responsive to what is going on in the regular classroom. Such responsiveness avoids duplication of content, accurately perceives what the basic instructional level in the school is, and encourages an extension of the individualized profile into the regular classroom.

Treffinger remarks that IEPs for the gifted and talented need to be concerned with the "unknown." He stresses that there must be an awareness that "very few 'solutions' are final" and that one task of the gifted is to deal with a future of complex, yet undefined, problems.

## The Home Factor

It is our belief that the parent is a largely overlooked member of the team. Parents need to be aware of the child's profile and style preferences in order to be realistic in planning future goals. Early conferences in which both educator and parent are free to discuss the child are an invaluable tool in refining prescriptions. Many such conferences confirm that the child's stylistic approach to both learning and life in general was evident from a very early age. Where enrichment and in some cases remediation is involved, the informed parent becomes another instructor. When school and home work together, there is less suspicion on both sides, and goals are attained more rapidly. For parents to be effective in the child's educational experience, they need to see accurately what the child is like, and what the school system is equipped to offer.

## Summing Up

Although we have pointed out specific approaches to dealing with the school and programming, we must note that there are no hard-and-fast rules. Common sense and flexibility may be your best assets. It may be better to "help" the school make changes slowly rather than to try to revolutionize the system. But there may be occasions when you cannot make any changes for your child within the system. In such instances you must either be patient and make the best of the situation, or seek out an alternative private facility.

We have seen many parents who have felt so "right" about what was necessary for a child that they antagonized the school staff. If, after getting several professional opinions on a problem, you still do not agree with anyone involved, perhaps it is time to reexamine your own motives in the matter. Many parents cannot accept reality where their children are concerned, and this refusal only makes a problem worse for the child.

Programming, evaluation, and IEPs are important aspects of your child's education. You need to be involved in planning without trying to appear the expert. You must be as accessible as necessary for everyone participating to get as clear a picture of your child's skills and personality as possible. Remember, the important thing is to keep the lines of communication open.

# 9
# *Developing the Potential*

This final chapter is something of a smorgasbord. In it we will discuss day-to-day enrichment, advocacy, parent organizations, and a variety of ordinary problems often encountered by parents of the gifted and talented. Remember that you, the parents, are a primary force in your children's education. Your expectations are a chief contributor to your children's level of motivation in academic areas. If you do not teach them to respect intellectual interests and learn frustration tolerance, as well as independence, than they may never reach their full potential.

## *Establishing a Home Atmosphere*

Many factors are involved in establishing a home atmosphere that is conducive to learning. Before we examine them specifically, let us talk about overall orientation.

An atmosphere that stimulates learning does not require elaborate paraphernalia or expensive extras. Learning is en-

encouraged when you take advantage of everyday occurrences to instruct your child. This does not mean that you must be lecturing at every turn, but it does suggest that you pay attention to situations that lend themselves to expansion. For example, let's say you are recovering one of your chairs with Naugahyde. Your child asks what that stuff is. You might reply that it is a fake leather. You could even mention in passing that another work for "fake" is imitation. The discussion could go on to an exploration of where leather and Naugahyde come from. You might try to identify other items in your home made of vinyl. The key to how far to expand the discussion is your child. Don't push the conversation to the point where he or she is yawning and glassy eyed, and you have laryngitis. When the child seems to lose interest, drop the subject. Remember not to use this technique every second of every day, since any technique, no matter now useful, loses its effect if overworked.

Books and magazines are important elements that encourage intellectual pursuits. If you spend a portion of your free time reading, your child will probably want to read for fun also. This doesn't mean that your house has to look like a branch of the public library, or that you must own all the books yourself. What books you do own are an asset, but the balance of your materials can come from the library. Start to familiarize your child with the library at as young an age as two or three. Even the few minutes you spend returning books are a worthwhile exposure. As soon as the child is old enough, take him or her to story hours and other activities the library offers, such as art exhibits. It does not matter that the works you view are by a local artist and not somebody famous. One learns to appreciate good art by seeing all kinds of products. Your local library, besides offering a selection of books and magazines, can contribute an added dimension to your child's cultural enrichment.

Another excellent habit to begin is talking to the child about what you are doing throughout the day. Don't worry about how much the child understands, or what people on the street think of your behavior. One woman who baby-sat with a toddler commented that people sometimes looked at her strangely because she carried on a running conversation with the child. She stated that conversation was something she had always had with her own children, and she intended to keep on doing it. She noted that such conversation had not hurt any of her own children, who all did very well in school.

Many parents of gifted children have demonstrated this kind of emphasis on verbal interaction. At first it is largely a one-way monologue, but as time goes on it becomes a true conversation. No subject is too trivial to discuss. When you talk about what color something is, what you are doing and in what order, or how big or how small something seems, you are enriching your child's world. Whether it is the characteristics of an object you point out or someone's motivations in performing some act, you have focused your child on conceptual thinking. Abstract labels like over, few, left, and equal become real for the child only when someone points out the connection between the label and the concrete meaning. We often assume that children pick up these conceptual labels on their own, but tests administered in kindergarten demonstrate that this is not true for a large percentage of our youngsters.

## Don't Ignore the Commonplace

Many ordinary items and home activities can provide opportunities for enrichment and education. Shopping and cooking offer a complex fabric of experiences that are beneficial to your child. Consider spices for a moment.

Condiments exhibit a variety of textures, colors, tastes, and smells that encourage discrimination and classification skills in the child. They originate from any number of exotic places, which will serve as still another avenue of information to explore. A good encyclopedia of cooking or a specialized cookbook often offers details on how foods like nutmeg are obtained, their importance, and how their use spread from place to place.

Just the act of measuring ingredients and combining diverse elements in one dish demonstrates to the child how the whole is often more than just the sum of its parts. What is cooking if not chemistry? Too often in our modern society, our children see only the prepackaged final product. Many items around them are too fragile, costly, and complicated for the child to take apart and reassemble. Cooking offers none of these difficulties. Not only does it enable children to learn sequence and how to follow directions, but it will bestow an intense satisfaction from producing something for themselves.

## Stimulating Environments

A stimulating environment is helpful not only for the gifted—the ideas suggested here would be beneficial to all children. Putting together a stimulating room need not be expensive or time consuming. Much can be accomplished with paint, ingenuity, and a good floor plan. Let us examine what helps constitute such enriching surroundings.

As parents we often have difficulty facing the fact that children are children and not miniature adults. Sometimes this is even more the problem with gifted children, who appear to be highly sophisticated. The fact is that children's tastes in general are very different from adults'. They don't like the same foods that adults savor and their preference in colors is also quite dissimilar.

Children are not intrigued with neutral colors as many adults are. Given a choice, they would not pick the pastels adults habitually select for them. They favor bright cheerful colors and bold prints. A can or two of paint may be just the thing to begin with.

As to furniture, the less there is, the better. If you can make do with a bed, a desk, a chair, and some other piece, you will be giving the child more room to play—and the child's needs are the primary consideration in setting up the room. Shelves and clothes hooks should be reachable, to encourage the child's independence.

The main criteria for floors and walls are durability, easy care, and easy use. It is difficult to build elaborate block structures on shag carpet, and creativity loses out if the room is for "show only." Children's rooms are for much more than sleeping; they serve many purposes. Children need room to play, dream, and experiment. Features like a section of wall covered with blackboard paint or a large roll of paper for drawing, set up on a rod to dispense like paper towels, give children the chance to express their ideas. When you plan your children's rooms, keep this in mind and avoid the stuffy, fussy, "look but don't touch" approach.

## The Value of Play

Toys that are more than just entertaining are of great value in shaping a child's learning skills. After all, play is more than a way to pass the time. It is through play and imagination that the child first learns to manipulate and experiment with the world.

In selecting toys for your child, let yourself be guided by two simple rules. First, learn to disregard the age ranges on toys and substitute your own common sense and a knowledge of your child. This does not mean you should buy for your two-year-old a toy designed for a twelve-year-old. It does mean that a box labeled for a five-year-old may well be suitable for your three-year-old. Manufacturers' labels on toys were not designed with the gifted child in mind. Gifted children are frequently interested in materials considered appropriate for a youngster several years older. Obviously you must watch out for safety features and supervise young children closely when they are playing with small parts. But learn to look beyond the manufacturer's conception of what is the best toy for a child your youngster's age.

Second, remember that in many instances the less the toy does itself, the better. (This does not rule out electronic games for children, but they fall into a separate category and should not be considered as part of the standard play materials.) Toys that allow multiple solutions and creative adaptations are the best. Old standbys like blocks and other construction materials, beads, paint, clay, discarded clothes, as well as simple figures of people and animals are the best stimulators of creativity. Toys that do too much are like TV. They produce passive, uninvolved children who expect others to do their thinking for them. Children love to make things themselves, and are intrigued with objects that can be adapted to a number of uses. How many times have you see children who are happier playing with the box an expensive gift came in rather than with the toy itself?

As the child gets older, you may want to investigate chemistry sets and construction materials with motorized parts. Just remember that these are items your child must "grow into" and the only way that can be done is to begin with simpler toys that utilize similar concepts.

Some families of gifted children share an intense interest in playing games. One family set aside a half hour a day for this purpose. Clearly, not every family can find that much time—you might be lucky to round up the members of your family once a week. The emphasis here is on quality and not quantity of time spent. Game playing not only offers fun and a chance to be together, but it also encourages thinking and skill development. From the simple ability to count and follow directions encountered in the most basic children's games to the complex challenges of chess, game playing fosters logical thought. Many of the qualities involved in being a good game player (such as forethought and planning) have an application in the academic sphere. Games can be either verbal or nonverbal in nature. Like Scrabble or Boggle, they can help develop vocabulary and reading skills. Games with a nonverbal emphasis focus on spatial elements like direction and size as well as on sequence and deductive reasoning.

### What about TV?

There is a strong controversy about how much, if any, TV children should be allowed to see. In a country where teen-agers rate TV watching right behind snacking as their favorite afternoon pursuit, it is a subject parents must confront.

TV can be a very relaxing entertainment for many people. Some of what is presented can also be thought provoking. However, we feel that parents should set clear limits on the amount and type of TV their children watch. In too many instances it has become an electronic baby-sitter that takes the responsibility of interacting with our children out of our hands. As a result, our preschoolers are programmed to expect school to have the same pace, scene shifts, and pure entertainment that TV provides. When the teacher can't do this, many children quickly lose interest in her presentation. Heavy TV watching turns children into passive creatures with no personal involvement in the learning process. When you are passive, it is difficult to muster the amount of energy necessary for more demanding pursuits such as reading. The more TV children watch the less they will be motivated to read. The content of the shows to which children are exposed should also be monitored. Programs of news content and others that stimulate discussion are preferable to shows emphasizing banal content or violence. However, you, the parent, are best suited to preview programs for suitability. Only you know what type of material you wish your children to see.

Controlling TV habits begins with the very young child. Whether a child is with a parent at home during the day or with a baby-sitter while the parents work outside the home, a very young child should watch little or no TV. Rather than being glued to a TV set, the toddler should be discovering the world. This does not mean that a confrontation with the child is inevitable. We have rarely told our small son, "You cannot watch TV"; rather, we have asked the baby-sitter to fill up his time with other activities, and have given her suggestions for doing so. At home we model the behavior we want from him. Seldom does he see us watch anything earlier than the evening news. Most often we are involved in hobbies or other activities that preclude TV. The result of our subtle modeling is that our son is more likely to turn off a TV playing in a room and hand the nearest adult a book to read to him than to sit down and watch a program.

Setting limits on TV viewing may not be difficult with your child. Although gifted and talented children are a diverse population, it is not uncommon for them to be disinterested in TV. They seem to want something more from things than just amusement. They frequently would rather dismantle toys to see how they work than play with them in the manner the manufacturer had in mind.

## Getting the Most from Books

One of the most underrated activities for parents and children may be sharing books aloud. When children are small, you read to them to give them exposure to language skills and for the companionship of simply being together. Once children start to read on their own (and for many gifted children this is quite young), the story time seems to go by the boards. That is too bad. Reading books is more than simply comprehending words and recognizing the plot and characters. Books are an opportunity to understand the subtleties of word play and human interactions. For example, you might ask your child why a character in the story was named "Mr. Glum." Try asking if the story would have ended differently if some major point of the tale was altered. You can even suggest that while most of the story itself may not change, the ending might be quite different. There are many versions of classic stories, such as the old nursery tale of the gingerbread boy. When reading a new story, ask the child to anticipate what is going to happen next or how the story will end. Always follow up with "why" questions, such as "Why was she bold? "Why did it fail?"

When selecting books, try to make sure that at least some of them are challenging. Left to their own devices many children will select works of high interest but low difficulty.

Many gifted children also get themselves into a rut on one subject. It doesn't hurt to suggest that at least one book they select at each library visit deal with some additional topic. Getting more from books than a good story requires some effort, but it is energy well invested.

## Teaching Decision Making

How many adults do you know who put off doing their holiday shopping until the last minute, not just because of the crowds but because they dread the ordeal of selecting the right present for the right person? One woman solved her problem by simply buying everything she thought her children would like, so that they would not be disappointed. Certainly this woman had other difficulties besides decision making, yet her case illustrates a problem in making choices that most of us encounter at one time or another.

Teaching decision making should being at an early age. We will present one method for accomplishing this goal. It is by no means the only method, but it will serve as an illustration of how to go about the task.

As you talk to the young child, you can discuss aloud why you are making certain choices, for example when you are buying his or her clothes. You might talk of price, color, size, or any of a number of other variables. Some time later you might in a similar situation present to the child two outfits *you* already find equally suitable. Let the child choose between them. Long before they can accurately label colors, children have their preferences. Continue in this manner, making adjustments as you go. If you are winding up with too many puppets, too much yellow, or too many ice cream pops, substitute another item for the favored one the next time you present the choice. What happens if the child changes his or her mind? That depends on *when* the change is made. If you are still "next to the rack" so to speak, let the substitution be made. Be careful to ask "Are you sure this is what you want?" If the change of mind begins after you've paid for the item and left, tell the child that you understand how he or she feels but that it is too late to go back. Remind the child whose choice it was, and that next time the other choice could be selected. Do not give in to tantrums. This is a common mistake parents commit. If you give in at this point, the child will learn nothing whatever about decision making, and everything about manipulating parents. As the child grows older, you can of course broaden the number of items to be selected from.

Of course, especially with a young child, people may regard you with amazement. One mother was in a crafts store with her small son, trying to select a picture to make for his room. Finally she presented him with two pictures and asked which one he liked better. He hesitated a few moments and then picked his favorite. A nearby saleswoman was taken aback. She asked the mother why she would bother to let a child so young select a picture. The boy's mother responded that it was his room and he should be happy with what was in it. Certainly the child was too young to have made a totally unscreened selection, but his mother was allowing him to make his first forays into decision making. Game playing also reinforces decision-making skills. A child who has grown up making choices will be pleased by the number and variety of decisions good games demand.

Encouraging a child to make decisions can also be helpful in gaining a child's cooperation. Rather than an unpleasant scene at bathtime, a question such as "Who will let out the bath-water, you or I?" can enlist the child's participation and fore-stall opposition. This technique works well in any number of parent/child interactions in which there is potential for con-flict, for example, eating and dressing.

Now, we cannot guarantee that teaching decision-making skills will keep you from wanting to rip your hair out when your adolescent decides to paint his or her room some ghastly shade. What it can do is to put a curb on impulsive behavior and allow the individual to make informed, reasoned choices. A child who has grown up experiencing the results of some poor choices may be a better decision maker as an adult.

## Developing Independence and Responsibility

Ask kindergarten teachers about the type of child they would least like to have in their classrooms and many of them will list immature, whiney youngsters. The best description of such children is "cute but helpless." Such children cling to adults. They may be very verbal but much of the talk seems to center around "I want" or similar instances of putting "I" before "you." Dependent children want instant compliance with their wishes. They do not want to share and may at times demand to be dressed from head to foot. Visualize the type of adolescents such children grow into: from helpless, cute, and irritating five-year-olds, they will become not-so-cute, self-centered, irresponsible, and aggravating teenagers. Parents sometimes fail to understand how they themselves help to create this unwanted behavior.

When children are young, we do everything for them because it is a necessity. As they get a little older we can either heed their signals for independence or stalwartly continue to function as their servants. For example, learning to feed oneself is a messy process. If you refuse to let the child participate when he or she first shows an interest, you begin subtly to reinforce feelings of ineptness. It's much faster to dress the child yourself than to let him or her make attempts at it, and sometimes it's necessary when you are under pressure, but as a day-to-day routine it can only reinforce dependency. Better to get up a little earlier or push bedtime back a few minutes to allow the child to experiment with dressing and undressing. At such moments it is best not to interfere with the process (no matter how slow and painful it may appear to the viewer) unless the child either asks for assistance or simply cannot do it unaided. We believe this is one of the most difficult phases in early attempts to encourage independence.

As parents, we are all too prone to speak for or translate for or do for our youngsters. But every time we take on the controlling role, the child falls back to being a dependent person. We are in fact reinforcing the behavior opposite to the one we desire. When nothing dangerous is involved, and the child says "I want to do it," let him or her try. The worst that comes from such attempts is a mess, and some lost time. What the child gains is a feeling of being believed in. First attempts are generally less than perfect, but the child may be more willing to let you show how to do the task better the next time, if you are tolerant of those initial disasters. Children without any disabilities should be fairly independent in self-help skills by the time they enter kindergarten.

Responsibility also begins at a very young age. While most people now feel that a house must be child-proofed from top to bottom, there is no reason to live in a barren environment for many years just because there are children in the house. Of course, dangerous substances and medicines should be under lock and key. The child's own room and some other place should be clear for unencumbered play. You could consider putting up a gate to your living or dining room rather than stripping everything bare. We do not believe that children should be allowed to be little tyrants, dictating every move their parents make. Developing a sense of responsibility means developing respect for the rights of others. It is not unfair to put one or two rooms off limits until the child is old enough to be around delicate or valuable things.

One mother handled this situation very well. From the time her daughter was an infant she would carry her around to look at or touch the "pretty" things. This session was a regular part of their routine, and as time went on the child was content to leave the objects alone unless her mother was with her.

Teaching children to care for their own toys is another way to teach responsibility. Do not rush out to replace a toy the minute your child breaks it. All youngsters gain from such behavior is instant gratification of their wishes and a distorted view of the value of things. When we complain about wasteful adults, we need to look to the behavior they learned as young children.

When children reach school age, independence and responsibility must extend into the classroom. If you continue to fight all their battles for them, you will find yourself selecting their college professors. The most common battleground for independence and responsibility is homework. Many parents seem to live in dread that a child will turn in less than perfect work. Sometimes they get so carried away with "helping" on a project that they wind up doing most of it. This holds true for the "helpless" teen as much as for the elementary school child. The same concept that applied to the preschooler's learning how to get dressed pertains to the school-age child. Doing too much for the child is not a good idea. It is not necessary, for instance, to check homework or contribute ideas. This does not mean remaining completely uninvolved. It does mean that children must take responsibility for their own work and that they will have to take the consequences for not getting the work in on time or for doing a poor job.

Both responsibility and independence require parents to trust their children. If you have taught them how to make decisions and encouraged them from an early age to do as much as possible for themselves, the chances are that you are rearing independent, responsible individuals.

## How to Ask a Question

There is an art to asking a question. Most of the time, we don't think about what we are asking and when our children don't give us the expected answer, we're all a bit confused. Watch what happens in this scenario:

Jack runs into the house. He is crying and upset. His father tries to find out what happened. The boy responds that Mike and Ken have been picking on him. His father asks, "Why do you think they did that?" His son answers, "Cause I saw them, that's why!"

What went wrong? Jack's father really wanted to know the reason for the fight, *not* whether Jack was sure of who was bullying him. Unfortunately he assumed that Jack could understand the implications of the word "why." Why is one of the most powerful words we have. It asks a person to think on an abstract level and to do some deductive reasoning. Young children whose view of cause-and-effect relationships is somewhat simplistic have more trouble responding to such an abstract query.

When you are asking a child questions that require complex answers, it is helpful to prompt with cues. This does not mean giving the child the answer. Try to lead the child step by step to give you the desired response. Social studies questions are a good place to try this technique because they frequently expect the child to recognize and understand some abstract principle. When you use a cue technique, it helps the child to break down a large, abstract concept into its component parts.

In addition, bear in mind when you are asking questions that facts are important, but that higher-order thinking skills need development as well. This is especially the case if you discuss stories with your children.

## Potpourri

As parents of gifted children, you may place undue pressures on yourself to ensure that your children produce. Of course, you may be putting undue pressures on your children as well. This is not necessary and often leads to alienated and rebellious children and adolescents. It is better to encourage your children by trying to understand them more thoroughly and by empathizing with their situation. Encourage by the use of discussions, but don't become a lecturer or a criticizer. Empathy, which is trying to feel what your children are feeling, is probably your best guide. If you can feel what they are experiencing, you are more likely to give sound advice and to be a real reinforcement to them in their endeavors. Too many parents try to make their children live the life the parents actually wanted for themselves. Don't let this happen to you. It usually backfires in the long run. If your children choose on their own a type of life-style or career that you've wanted for them, all the better, but don't push in certain directions just because it will make you feel better. As parents of gifted and talented children, you need to examine your own motivations carefully. Do not let the good fortune of living with such children go to your head.

One example of thoughtless behavior with respect to the gifted is the tendency of parents to brag. When you brag or show off your children, it will lead them to develop certain personality characteristics other people will dislike. Remember, the way you present yourself today will be the way your children will present themselves eventually. Your children are human beings first, who also happen to be gifted or talented. They need to behave in a manner that would be appropriate for any other person. Teaching them snobbery and superciliousness will not help them to get along in the world. Furthermore, regardless of their ability level, children—like everyone else—need to feel loved for themselves and not for their accomplishments.

This is especially important to remember when only one child in a family of several children is gifted or talented. Follow the philosophy of treating all the children equally and as important individuals. Emphasize that each of us has certain things we can do better than others. Acknowledge the child's gift but don't worship the ability. Being gifted or talented does not make one a better person. If you want to avoid conflicts that may ensue in such a family, avoid favoritism. Secretly you may find one of the children more pleasing, but try to suppress the urge to express this feeling. Favoring one child because he or she is gifted or talented is destructive to that child's future development. Try to help each child discover and value the talents of brothers and sisters. Sometimes it is harder to do this when the gifted one is the youngest and seems to outdo the other youngsters at every turn. This is the time to assign privilege according to age, so that an older child can feel important as well. When the gifted one is the oldest, you may have to sympathize with the younger children, because all their teachers may insist on comparing them with their older sibling. It is difficult to have to go through life in your brother's or sister's shadow. Love all of your children for themselves and not for an IQ level or a special talent.

# Advocacy

An advocacy group is one formed to support a cause. We will discuss further on the details of forming and operating a parent's advocacy group for the gifted and talented. For now let us look at some pitfalls to avoid.

Advocacy groups tend to form only when there is a crisis to spark people into action. But like medicine, advocacy is at its best when it is preventive in nature and not reactive. Why? Because groups that form in the heat of anger frequently are both irrational and short-lived. A good advocacy group, like a good program, is organized and logical and has clearly set-out goals. If it is formed well before a crisis breaks, it will have time to develop a positive image. You would be surprised how many parent groups get slapped with labels like "hotheads," "radicals," and "troublemakers." Let us investigate further.

## What's Wrong with the Emotional Approach

Many parents, especially when they feel their child has been shortchanged, want to rush into school and take out their frustrations on the first staff member they encounter. While at a gut level we can empathize with these feelings, such behavior is, at best, meaningless. At its worst it will convince both the school and other parents that such a parent is self-centered and shortsighted and has a few screws loose.

When people react in irrational ways, they also tend to become rigid in their views. This is anathema when dealing with a school system. Irrational parents distrust any compromise that is offered by administrators, believing that it is probably a further method of cheating them and their child of their rights. They may resort to bullying tactics, hoping that a show of aggression and determination will frighten the administration into doing things their way. Muscle replaces logic, and in such cases parents may lose the ability to present their case to its best advantage. Rarely does intimidation of this type work. Administrators, if they don't simply throw you off the grounds, will yes you to death and then do just as they please. You will also derive little benefit from going over one administrator's head to another before you have exhausted all possibilities with the first. Such high-handed behavior will only create more animosity toward you and your cause. You may think that you will get more results by going to the top, but upper administration will probably not make any move before they investigate the situation completely. With the emotional approach you feel better initially, but wind up with ulcers and high blood pressure before a solution is reached, if one ever is reached short of court action.

## How Not to Start a Group

Parent groups work best and are more prone to survival when they are a team effort. If you envision yourself a bold general leading the charge—forget it! Look, for example, at successful fraternal and hobby groups. Those that are popular involve a large number of their members in a significant amount of activity and decision making. The minute the leadership of such groups falls into the hands of a static little band, unrest begins and participation starts to drop off. Like any conglomerate of individuals, from the small community group to the total voting public, when people feel powerless they become apathetic. Just because starting the parent group was your idea, there is no need to become a petty despot. Share the leadership of your advocacy group or you will find yourself the captain of a ghost ship.

## You Are Not in It Alone

A common complaint about advocacy groups is that they have a keen sense of territory and refuse to work with similar orgnizations on common goals. Such a group may act as if it were the most important association around, as if it had the only pipeline to the latest and best information on the subject. The cause that initially drew the members together seems to be forgotten in the tug of war with other groups for regional power. It is upsetting to see this happen to people who began with the best intentions in the world. It is also upsetting when you realize that it is the children who will suffer in the end. When a group becomes short-sighted, its goals focus on one-upmanship rather than on accomplishing change for the children's sakes. The result is a lot of little splinter groups that spend their time hissing at each other during legislative hearings, which does nothing to enhance the image of an already less than popular cause. Once you realize that your group is an unofficial chapter of a national movement, you will gain a clearer perspective. Two of the best-know national organizations for the gifted and talented are The Association for the Gifted (TAG), The Council for Exceptional Children, 1920 Association Drive, Reston, Virginia 22091; and the National Association for Gifted Children, 217 Gregory Drive, Hot Springs, Arkansas 71901.

Many people believe that affiliating their local group with a national organization will dispel infighting. While we have no proof that this method works, it's an idea worth considering. Remember, there is power in unity.

## Look to Past Models of Success

An advocacy group for the gifted and talented is certainly at a disadvantage because of the swings of public interest in the gifted and talented as an educational subdivision. Therefore, it is probably better to look for model organizations that are already successful in moving legislators to action. Probably the most successful educational advocacy groups of late have been those involved with the handicapped. Recently, organizations supporting legislation for the learning disabled have also been effective. Like the gifted and talented, learning-disabled children are a diverse category that are not easily described. Parents of learning-disabled children have fought a long uphill battle to gain appropriate services for these youngsters. A neophyte gifted and talented organization should take a good long look at how learning disabilities associations in their community have dealt with the educational establishment.

Unfortunately, gifted and talented organizations will infrequently have the kind of backing that a special education parent-teacher association (SEPTA) offers to parents of the learning disabled. Many special education groups want no part of the gifted and talented, for fear that scarce financial support will be spread even more thin. Unfortunately, too, no assurance can be offered that their worst fears will not be justified.

## Educate Your Membership

Before you get much past the basic organizational phase, you should begin to assess how much your membership knows about gifted and talented education. Try to be honest. Few people, even well-educated professionals, will necessarily be well versed in educational theory. Start a workshop program and bring in guest speakers. Continually upgrade the level of awareness of everyone involved in your group.

You cannot fight for something as abstract as an educational concept if you don't understand it. Even in noneducational groups, membership ignorance can be deadly to the organization. With a portion of your dues, work to purchase books and periodicals that can serve as a lending library for the members. Many books are hard to obtain and your members will be glad to avoid searching hither and yon for them.

## Should We Start a Newsletter?

While newsletters are a nice touch, they are not cheap to produce, and they require devoted workers who are willing to put in long hours on a regular basis. Newsletters are not a good way to start. They work best in medium- to large-size groups, where it is hard to keep in touch. Initially, and maybe for quite some time, your group will probably not be of a size to balance a newletter's advantages with the aggravation of getting it out. If, however, your membership is spread over a large geographical area, then a newsletter may be your only link with group's current interests. The best judge will have to be your organization. Don't try to paint too rosy a picture of what "fun" a newsletter is; you may find yourself doing all the work.

## Appropriate Goals

The key to success for your group will most likely lie in realistic goals. Remember the IEP? It has short-term goals and long-term goals. The same should apply to your organization.

A first-level goal should be to assess how the district and community feel about education for the gifted and talented. Trace lines of command and policies on early admission, grade skipping, homogeneous grouping, and other technical points. Go to several school board meetings and see where the power base is. Try to find out whether those individuals are favorably disposed toward gifted and talented education or could become interested in it. Don't make any rash decisions. It is more important to go slowly and understand the unique system you are working with than to ruin everything with one ill-conceived move.

You may need initially to settle for some small offerings. If you can get the district to assess numbers and develop identification criteria, you should be more than pleased. Sometimes it takes a couple of years to get from these early planning stages to an operational program.

Try to encourage both your members and the district to "think small." Sometimes to look good and to get parents to stop badgering, districts launch grandiose schemes. They believe that such a program will satisfy the general public that they have tried and are doing something. If it doesn't work out, they can shrug their shoulders and say "too bad." By their very size, such projects are doomed to failure. If you have never designed and run a one-shot, kindergarten-to-twelfth-grade program, you have virtually no chance of making it a success.

Parents, on the other hand, are prone to the view that if they don't get everything *now* they'll wind up with nothing. Sometimes it is this type of parent pressure that pushes school districts into ill-designed programs. The district's other possible reaction to nonnegotiable terms is to give you nothing right from the start. Then you are worse off than when you started; not only do you not have a program, but you have incurred the district's wrath on the mere mention of the topic. The choice is yours. Set realistic goals and you will achieve some satisfaction for your efforts.

## Are Advisory Committees Useful?

Advisory committees are set up by districts to gather information cheaply on topics that the school board or upper administration wishes to know more about. They can also be a handy way to pacify unhappy taxpayers. Whether the advisory committee in your district turns out to be helpful will be determined as much by the district's intentions as by the members' ability to produce useful information.

Some districts give their committees more authority than do others. For instance, members of an advisory committee might have a representative on an appeals group or be involved in interviewing. A similar group in another district may be encouraged only to look for grant money. The choice is really the district's. The members of an advisory committee may eventually, however, form the nucleus of a parents' organization.

## Ploys School Districts Use

Once your group is formed, you must be ready to deal with the various strategies that will be used to counter your requests. A favorite opening gambit is to shrug one's shoulders and say, "Nice idea, too bad there's no money." Especially in these times of economic stringency, that would seem a perfect response. However, it's a dodge. Remember, you are starting small. You could suggest an early admissions procedure. Where the district has no preschool testing program, parents could always seek private evaluation. Where no kindergarten screening is used, suggest it. Such screening is relatively inexpensive, and would identify handicapped as well as gifted students.

Propose some change of class grouping, or content acceleration, or a variety of other things that do not cost a lot. Keep your facts straight. With accurate data to back your suggestions and little cost to the district in money, the administration may be willing to begin a pilot program.

Another favorite stall is "We need time to study the problem." Some districts have been studying the problem for years. This might be the point at which to suggest an advisory committee to help the district acquire information, develop goals, and establish a commitment. Here again it might be helpful to arrive with a list of information sources and material on how to develop gifted and talented programs.

Both of the foregoing situations are relatively simple ones. The really difficult districts declare "We are the experts and we will do what's best." When you get this response you will need public pressure to change anyone's mind. This pressure will come about only if you have already established a base in the community. Community pressure can help elect board of education members who are favorable to gifted and talented programming. It can suggest to the administrators that there is a real demand in the community for such programs, rather than their being the concern of one or two pushy parents.

## A Reminder

When you form an advocacy group, your chief goal is to advance the interests of gifted and talented children. Secondary goals are the education of the membership and mutual support. The reason we stress the sequence of goals is that too many groups get bogged down in the social and support aspects of the organization. Because so many groups organize around problems, they have a natural tendency to ruminate over injustices. Avoid the tendency to continue this problem sharing long past the point where it is useful to anyone. Instead, channel your energy into dealing with the system, influencing political leaders, setting up children's workshops, and other positive long- and short-term goals. Immediately following this chapter is a copy of the constitution and bylaws of a parent advocacy group, which is typical of the type of document many associations develop. You may find it a useful example in helping your group develop its own guidelines.

## Summing Up

We have emphasized in this chapter and throughout the book the importance of parents in the education and development of their children. Parenting is a heavy responsibility, and no one has yet found perfect parents or the ideal way of raising children. Parents are human beings first and are entitled to make mistakes. The important factor in good parenting is sincerity. If you are willing to work for the very best for your child, you will probably succeed regardless of the mistakes you make along the way. It may seem strange to write a parents' manual at a time when society is demanding more and more from government agencies and other institutions. However, we feel it is important to support the family, which in reality carries the most weight in making a difference for today's children.

# Constitution and Bylaws for a Parent Advocacy Group

## Article I—Name

This organization shall be a non-profit organization and shall be called the Suffolk County Coordinating Council for the Education of Gifted and Talented.

## Article II—Purposes

The purposes of the Council shall be:

1. To provide a forum for the development of public awareness of the needs of the gifted and talented;

2. To serve as an interchange of information on the subject of gifted and talented;

3. To develop cooperation with community and professional organizations;

4. To provide an organized "voice" for parents, teachers, administrators, school board members and others concerned with the unmet needs of the gifted and talented.

Reprinted with permission of the Suffolk County (New York) Coordinating Council for the Education of the Gifted and Talented.

## Article III—Membership

Membership in the Council shall be open to all persons interested in the purposes of the Council upon payment of dues as provided herein.

A member in good standing is a member whose dues for the current year are paid.

## Article IV—Dues

Dues shall be payable annually in October for the ensuing year. The dues shall be in an amount set by the Executive Board and approved by the membership at regular meetings. In the event the amount set by the Executive Board for any year is not approved, the dues shall be the same as those last approved by the membership.

## Article V—Annual Meeting

The regular meeting in August or September shall be known as the annual meeting and shall be for the purpose of electing trustees, receiving reports of officers and committees, and for any other business that may arise.

## Article VI—Trustees and Their Duties

A. There shall be a Board of Trustees consisting of five members who shall be elected as trustees by the members of the Council as provided in Article XI hereof. Said trustees shall be elected at each annual meeting and shall hold office until the next annual meeting and until successor trustees shall have been elected and qualified.

B. The Board of Trustees shall establish and be responsible for the execution of its policies and shall supervise the activities of the Executive Board in order that the objectives and purposes of this Council may be fulfilled.

C. The Board of Trustees shall meet at least once a year at the annual meeting of the Council to appoint the president.

D. Three members of the Board of Trustees shall constitute a quorum for the transaction of business. No voting by proxy shall be permitted.

E. At the first meeting of the Board of Trustees after its election, the Board shall elect a chairperson and a secretary to conduct the Board's business for the term of its election.

F. The Board of Trustees may appoint one of its members as president of the Council.

G. Any vacancy on the Board of Trustees shall be filled by an election by the Executive Board of the Council, and said trustee elected thereby shall serve out the remainder of the term left vacant.

## Article VII—Officers

1. Officers: The officers of this Council shall be president, vice president, recording secretary, corresponding secretary and treasurer. Said officers, except the president, shall be appointed at the annual meeting by the president. In the event the Board of Trustees is unable or fails to appoint a president of this Council at the time of the annual meeting, then the Board of Trustees shall appoint a vice president to assume the duties of the president until a president is appointed. At said annual meeting, a special committee shall be appointed by the Board of Trustees for the purpose of seeking a qualified person or persons who shall be suitable for the office of president and whose name it shall submit to the Board of Trustees.

### Duties of the Officers

1. The President shall:
   a. preside at all meetings of the Council and at all Executive Board meetings.
   b. be ex-officio member of all committees, except the nominating committee referred to in Article XI hereof.
   c. countersign all checks, signed by the treasurer and approved by the Executive Board or as provided in the budget.
   d. appoint the chair of all the committees, both standing and special.
   e. remove committee chairs with the consent of the Executive Board.
   f. perform all the other duties pertaining to the office, and entrusted by the Board of Trustees, in order that the objectives and purposes of this Council may be fulfilled.
2. The Vice President shall:
   a. assume the duties of the president, in the absence of or at the request of the president.
   b. perform those functions which the president shall direct.
3. The Recording Secretary shall:
   record the minutes of all regular and Executive Board meetings of the Council and perform such other duties as may be directed by the president of the Executive Board.
4. The Corresponding Secretary shall:
   a. Send or cause to be sent, to all members, the proper notice of all membership meetings
   b. Send or cause to be sent, to all members of the Executive Board proper notice of all Executive Board meetings.
   c. perform all other functions directed by the president of the Executive Board.

5. The Treasurer shall:
   a. receive and deposit all monies of the Council.
   b. disburse such sums as provided by the budget or as voted by the Executive Board or the membership.
   c. keep an accurate record of receipts and expenditures.
   d. present a brief financial statement at every regular meeting of the membership and also at Executive Board meetings if requested.
   e. make a detailed financial report at the annual meeting.
   f. perform all other functions as directed by the president.

## Article VIII—Executive Board

1. Duties:
   A. Except as otherwise provided in this Constitution, the Executive Board shall have the power to transact the business of the Council.
   B. The Executive Board shall consist of the president, the vice president, the recording secretary, the treasurer, and any others deemed necessary by the president.
   C. Each officer and each committee chairperson shall have one vote on any one issue.
   D. There shall be no voting by proxy.
   E. In the event that there is a vice-chairperson of a standing committee, only the chairperson has the right to vote. In the absence of the chairperson, the vice-chairperson shall have the right to vote.
   F. In no case shall any one member have more than one vote on any one issue.
   G. Budget:
      1. The Executive Board shall present to the membership for its approval an annual budget for the period October 1 through the following September 30. This budget shall be presented at the August or September meeting prior to the budget.
      2. In the event the budget is not approved at this meeting, the Executive Board shall proceed forthwith to present an acceptable budget.
   H. In the event a budget is not approved by the membership, the Executive Board shall have the authority to spend not in excess of $1,000.00 per month without the approval of the membership.
   I. In the event that a committee chairperson has been absent for three consecutive Executive Board meetings, the president shall, with the approval of the Executive Board, replace her/him with another chairperson.
   J. The Executive Board shall meet once every month unless otherwise voted by the Board.

K. The Executive Board shall arrange for an annual audit of the books of the treasurer.

## Article IX—Standing Committees

1. The standing committees may be as provided herein or as otherwise deemed necessary by the Executive Board.

| | |
|---|---|
| Community Action | Planning and Finance |
| Curriculum | Program |
| Hospitality | Publicity |
| Information Clearinghouse | Research |
| Legislative Action | Saturday Workshop |
| Library | Activities |
| Membership Participation | Scholarship |
| Newsletter | Ways and Means |

2. The chairs of the standing committees shall present general plans of work to the Executive Board for approval. No action shall be taken until the general plans are approved. Upon approval of such plans, the committee shall take charge of and execute them. The committee shall execute other instructions that may be given it by the Executive Board.

## Article X—Meetings

1. Dates:
   A. Regular meetings of this Council shall be held at least three times a year, unless otherwise provided by the membership of the Executive Board.
   B. In the event a meeting date is changed, at least ten days notice of said new meeting date must be given to the membership.

## Article XI—Elections and Terms of Office

1. Nominations:
   A. Nominating Committee: A nominating committee of three members shall be appointed annually in the first quarter of the year by the Executive Board. The nominating committee shall prepare a slate of trustees to be presented at the regular meeting of the Council prior to the annual meeting and at the annual meeting.
   B. Nominations will be accepted from the floor at both these meetings.
   C. The corresponding secretary shall notify the membership of the slate of proposed trustees before the regular meeting prior to the annual meeting.

D. Members of the nominating committee may be nominated for trustees.
2. All trustees and officers shall serve for one year from annual meeting to annual meeting and until their successors shall have been elected and appointed. They may be reelected and reappointed to serve consecutive terms.

## Article XII—Vacancies in Office

1. In the event that a vacancy arises in any office other than that of the president, the vacancy shall be filled by the Executive Board.
2. In the event that there is a vacancy in the office of the president, those provisions applying to the appointment of president shall be followed. (See Article VI)

## Article XIII—Amendments

1. This Constitution and Bylaws may be amended by a two-thirds vote of the members voting, a quorum being present, provided that this amendment has been presented in writing to every member in good standing at least ten days before the meeting at which the vote is to be taken.
2. When a motion to amend is properly before the membership, it shall be the duty of the corresponding secretary to provide the notice in writing to the members.
3. In order to properly place a motion to amend this Constitution before the membership, the following steps must be taken:
   A. A motion must be made at a regular meeting.
   B. This motion must be approved by five other members in good standing.
   C. This motion and the approval of the five other members must be presented to the recording secretary.
   D. This motion shall then be tabled until the next regular meeting or until a special meeting for its consideration shall be called. At this meeting, proper notice having been given, it shall be read, discussed and voted upon.

## Article XIV—Rules of Order

Roberts' Rules of Order, as most recently revised, shall be the authority for procedures in all cases in which they are applicable, and in which they are not inconsistent with these Bylaws.

# Glossary

**APGAR Score** The physician's check-sheet score for evaluating the physical condition of newborn infants.

**Acceleration** *See* Content Acceleration; Early Admission; Early Graduation; Grade Skipping.

**Advocacy** The act of supporting something, such as a cause.

**Affective Training** Teaching children to deal with feelings, values, and social interactions.

**Authoritarianism** The use of a high degree of control, as in child rearing.

**Average** On Wechsler's classification system, an IQ score between 90 and 109.

**Basal** The point on a test when the child gets everything right.

**Behavioral (Guilford)** Behavioral skills are what Guilford calls "social intelligence." These are skills involved in accurate perception of people and their motivation. Behavioral skills are part of Contents.

**Bloom's Taxonomy** A grouping of learning skills from concrete and basic to highly abstract.

**Bright Normal** On Wechsler's classification system, an IQ score between 110 and 119. Currently called high average.

**Broad Search** A term often used as synonymous with divergent ability.

**Ceiling** On tests in general, the upper limit containing the most difficult questions. On the Stanford-Binet, L-M, ceiling also refers to the age level at which the child does not pass any task.

**Centralized Pullout** A resource-room class not located in the student's home school. Usually is a center to which children are bused from around a district.

**Chronological Age** The actual age of the child, usually stated in years, months, and days.

**Classes (Guilford)** Dividing information into groups or sets; considered a product skill by Guilford.

**Cluster** A group of children of similar ability placed together in an otherwise heterogeneous classroom.

**Cognition (Guilford)** Comprehension of the environment. Cognition is considered part of Operations by Guilford.

**Conceptual Sorting** The act of placing information into groups, sets, or classes.

**Content Acceleration** A type of acceleration that gives the child more advanced subject matter without necessarily changing class placement.

**Contents (Guilford)** The four types of information that are processed. *See also* Behavioral; Figural; Semantic; Symbolic.

**Convergent (Guilford)** Finding the one best right way of solving problems. Sometimes referred to as the "school block" of abilities. Considered an Operation by Guilford.

**Cutoff Score** The score (either group or individual) for IQ and/or achievement below which a student is rejected for a gifted or talented program.

**Direct Entry** The admission of a child into a program without further scrutiny when the child's scores meet or exceed cutoff standards.

**Divergent (Guilford)** Examining many different solutions to problems. Stress is on variety and quantity. Sometimes considered synonymous with "broad search." Divergent skills are considered part of Operations by Guilford.

**Early Admission** Allowing a child younger than the usually required age to enroll in either kindergarten or first grade.

**Early Graduation** Leaving the regular public school system some time earlier than usual.

**Elaboration** The ability to add detail, additional reasons, or other enrichment of things or information.

**Enrichment** Usually refers to exposing children to cultural and other information that will help them to expand their skills.

**Enrichment Triad (Renzulli)** A model for educating and evaluating gifted children. It has three levels: General Exploratory Experiences; Group Training Activities; Individual and Small Group Investigation of Real Problems.

**Equivalent Data** Test or other evaluation data that can be submitted in place of the criteria used by the schools for admittance into a special program.

**Evaluation (Guilford)** The ability to make judgements about information or situations. Considered to be part of Operations by Guilford.

**Expressive Vocabulary** The range and sophistication of the vocabulary the child actually uses.

**Figural (Guilford)** One of the four types of information that are processed. Consists of perceptual material. Considered part of Contents by Guilford.

**Flexibility** The ability to shift and see alternate methods, alternate answers, and so forth.

**Fluency** The ability to give a number of responses in a situation or to a stimulus.

**Frustration Tolerance** The ability to stay with a task and attempt to complete it despite whatever difficulties and obstacles may occur.

**Functioning Level** The actual academic level at which a child is performing at the time of the testing.

**Genius** A person who has created a major production, such as a symphony or a book, of original and lasting social value.

**Gifted** Having the potential to achieve eminence and/or produce something of lasting social value.

**Grade Skipping** Advancing the child from the current grade level to a placement at least one year beyond where other children of a similar age are placed.

**Heterogeneous Grouping** A grouping system in which a wide range of abilities is present.

**Homogeneous Grouping** A grouping system in which all the children are functioning on a similar academic level. In a gifted group all the children would be functioning at least 2 to 3 years above grade level.

**IEP** Individual Educational Plan. A system to design academic material tailored to the unique needs of each child.

**IQ** Intellectual Quotient. Any of a number of scores on intellectual testing that purport to indicate the present level of the child's intellectual functioning.

**Identification** (1) The process of developing a strong sense of self through modeling. (2) The process of determining which children are to be called gifted and talented.

**Immediate Rote Recall** The ability to remember material after one presentation, either visual or auditory.

**Implications (Guilford)** A highly abstract set of skills at the Products level, often associated with creativity. Implications skills are those involved in tasks such as hypothesis development.

**Individual Differences** The qualities that make each person unlike all others, with an emphasis on noting unique characteristics.

**Individualized Basics (Treffinger)** A review of a child's basic skills in any subject area with the intention of remediating any deficits.

**Itinerant Teacher** A teacher who services two or more schools, traveling between them.

**Labeling** The ability to call something by its correct name.

**Learning Style** (1) The intellectual pattern evidenced on testing. (2) The manner of instruction, such as small group, individual contact, lecture, and so forth.

**Long-Term Retrieval** The ability to remember something that was learned in the past.

**Matrix** A method by which test scores and opinion are weighed and then totaled, to determine a cutoff level for entrance into a program.

**Memory (Guilford)** The ability to recall material that has been learned in the past. *See also* Immediate Rote Recall; Long-Term Retrieval.

**Mental Age** The age equivalent that the child's performance on an intelligence test most closely resembles.

**Mentor** An individual, frequently an older child, who works with an advanced youngster in a specific subject or on a specific topic or project.

**Modeling** The emulation of the feelings or behavior of one individual by another.

**Motivation** The individual's level of desire to perform a specific task or tasks.

**Narcissistic** Being concerned with oneself to the exclusion of the needs or desires of others.

**Norm** A chart or charts that state at what levels a performance can be considered average, superior, and so forth.

**Normal Curve** A statistical and pictorial representation of the norm charts.

**Nurture** The effect of the environment on an individual.

**Operations (Guilford)** The major intellectual processes. *See also* Cognition; Convergent; Divergent; Evaluation; Memory.

**Overachiever** A child who is thought to be performing above his or her intellectual potential. There is *no* such thing as an overachiever.

**Percentile** A rating of test performance that ranges from 1 to 99. The higher the percentile, the better the performance. The fiftieth percentile is average.

**Precocious** Referring to a child who performs some act at a considerably earlier age than one would expect.

**Products (Guilford)** The organization of information to be processed. *See also* Classes; Implications; Relations; Systems; Transformations; Units.

**Pullout Program** *See* Centralized Pullout; Resource Room.

**Reliability** The ability of a test to produce similar performances in the same person on several different administrations.

**Receptive Vocabulary** The range and sophistication of the vocabulary that the child understands.

**Relations (Guilford)** Relations skills involve tasks such as comparing and contrasting concepts. Relations are considered part of Products by Guilford.

**Renzulli's Triad** *See* Enrichment Triad (Renzulli).

**Resource Room** A place in the child's home school where special program services are provided.

**Revolving Door (Renzulli)** Renzulli's system of rotating children into and out of gifted and talented programs.

**SOI** *See* Structure of Intellect (Guilford).

**School Block of Ability** A set of skills most often associated with school tasks. Often considered synonymous with Convergent Ability.

**Self-Concept** One's view of oneself and one's competence.

**Semantic (Guilford)** The ability to process the meanings we connect with words. Semantic skills are considered part of Contents by Guilford.

**Short-Term Memory** *See* Immediate Rote Recall.

**Sibling(s)** The brothers and sisters in a family.

**Sight Vocabulary** The number of words a child can recognize and read on sight.

**Significant** Referring to a result that has not occurred merely by chance alone.

**Skill Profile** *See* Learning Style (1).

**Standard Deviation** The way in which scores are distributed on the normal curve.

**Standard Error of Measurement** The degree of inaccuracy of a test score.

**Stanine** A rating of test performance, which ranges from 1 to 9. The higher the stanine the better the performance.

**Structure of Intellect (Guilford)** Called SOI by Guilford's followers. A theory that postulates that intelligence is multifactored.

**Superior** On Wechsler's classification system, an IQ score between 120 and 129.

**Symbolic (Guilford)** Symbolic skills deal with denotative signs, which do not have any meaning in themselves. Symbolic skills are considered part of Contents by Guilford.

**Systems (Guilford)** The ability to understand and analyze complex sets of information, as in problem solving.

**Tactile** Referring to the sense of touch.

**Talented** Children with great skill in a specific area, as opposed to general academic ability.

**Taxonomy** A grouping or classification system presented as a hierarchy.

**Test Floor** On tests in general, the lower limit containing the easiest questions. *See also* Basal.

**Transformations (Guilford)** Flexibility or the ability to shift. It is considered part of Products by Guilford. It is a very abstract skill, often associated with creativity.

**Underachiever** A child whose academic performance is below what one would expect based on age, grade and IQ.

**Units (Guilford)** A specific circumscribed piece of information, such as vocabulary. Considered part of Products by Guilford.

**Validity** The ability of a test actually to measure what it purports to measure.

**Very Superior** On Wechsler's classification system, an IQ score at or above 130.

**Vocabulary** *See* Expressive Vocabulary; Receptive Vocabulary; Sight Vocabulary.

**Weighed Score** The amount of points (and importance) assigned to a test score, rating, and so forth, when used in a matrix system.

**Williams' Cube Model** A model that interrelates curriculum, teacher behavior, and pupil behavior for individual programming.

# Selected Bibliography

This bibliography encompasses works cited in the text as well as many additional books, articles, and periodicals. An attempt has been made to select the most up-to-date sources wherever possible. We have divided the bibliography into three levels: Level A consists of introductory book and magazines suitable for the beginning reader; Level B has intermediate level books and journals, some of a fairly complex nature, which require a familiarity with the subject; and Level C is made up mostly of fairly complex theory and research books and journals, suitable for professionals or those with extensive backgrounds in gifted and talented education.

These divisions are not meant to be absolute. We designed the system to allow you, the reader, to progress at your own pace. Many of the references are listed in *Handbook of Instructional Resources and References for Teaching the Gifted*, by Karnes and Collins (16), who also list older material. To get the most out of this bibliography, you may want to use it in conjunction with the Karnes/Collins listing, which is annotated.

## Level A

1. Abraham, W. et al. *Gifts, Talents and the Very Young.* National/State Leadership Training Institute on the Gifted and the Talented, Ventura County Superintendent of Schools, 535 E. Main St., Ventura, CA 93009, 1977.

2. Baskin, Barbara H., and Harris, Karen H. *Books for the Gifted Child.* New York: R. R. Bowker, 1980.

3. Boston, B., ed. *Resource Manual of Information on Gifted Education.* Reston, VA: Council for Exceptional Children, 1975.

4. Brumbaugh, F.N., and Roscho, B. *Your Gifted Child.* New York: Henry Holt & Co., 1959.

5. Coffee, K., et al. *Parents Speak on Gifted and Talented Children.* Ventura, CA: National/State Leadership Training Institute on the Gifted and the Talented, Ventura County Superintendent of Schools, 1976.

6. Delp, J., and Martinson, R. *The Gifted and Talented: A Handbook For Parents.* Ventura, CA: National/State Leadership Training Institute on the Gifted and the Talented, Ventura County Superintendent of Schools, 1975.

7. Dennis, W., and Dennis, M., eds. *The Intellectually Gifted: An Overview.* New York: Grune and Stratton, 1976.

8. Dickinson, R. *Caring for the Gifted.* North Quincy, MA: Christopher, 1970.

9. Fortna, R., and Boston, B. *Testing the Gifted Child: An Interpretation in Lay Language.* Reston, VA: Council for Exceptional Children, 1976.

10. *G/C/T* (Gifted/Creative/Talented Children). G/C/T Publishing Co., Box 66654, Mobile, AL 36606. $15/yr.

11. *Gifted Children Newsletter.* Gifted and Talented Publications, Inc., 1255 Portland Place, Boulder, CO 80323. Monthly. $12.

12. Ginsberg, G., and Harrison, C. *How to Help Your Gifted Child: A Handbook for Parents and Teachers.* New York: Monarch, 1977.

13. Grost, Audrey. *Genius in Residence.* Englewood Cliffs, NJ: Prentice-Hall, 1971.

14. Hall, Eleanor G., and Skinner, Nancy. *Somewhere to Turn: Strategies for Parents of the Gifted and Talented.* New York: Teachers College Press, Columbia University, 1980.

15. Kanigher, H. *Everyday Enrichment for Gifted Children at Home and School.* Ventura, CA: National/State Leadership Training Institute on the Gifted and the Talented, Ventura County Superintendent of Schools, 1977.

16. Karnes, F.A., and Collins, E.C. *Handbook of Instructional Resources and References for Teaching the Gifted.* Boston: Allyn and Bacon, 1980.

17. Kaufman, F. *Your Gifted Child and You.* Reston, VA: Council for Exceptional Children, 1976.

18. Khatena, Joe. *The Creatively Gifted Child: Suggestions for Parents and Teachers.* New York: Vantage Press, 1978.

19. Krueger, M. *On Being Gifted.* New York: Walker, 1978.

20. Lawless, R. *A Guide for Educating a Gifted Child in Your Classroom.* Buffalo, NY: Disseminators of Knowledge, 1976.

21. Montour, Kathleen. "American Prerevolutionary Prodigies." *Intellectually Talented Youth Bulletin* 2, no. 9 (May 15, 1976).

22. Montour, Kathleen. "William James Sidis: The Broken Twig." *American Psychologist* 32, no. 4 (April, 1977): 265–279.

23. Newman, E., ed. *Reaching Out: Advocacy for the Gifted and Talented.* New York: Teachers College Press, Columbia University, 1980.

24. "The Story of the Sad Bear." *The Journal of Creative Behavior* 14, no. 2 (1980).

25. Strang, R. *Helping Your Gifted Child.* New York: Dutton, 1960.

26. Tuttle, F.B., and Becker, L.A. *Characteristics and Identification of Gifted and Talented Students.* Washington, DC: National Education Association, 1980.

27. Vail, P.L. *The World of the Gifted Child.* New York: Walker, 1979.

# LEVEL B

28. Boston, B. ed. *Gifted and Talented: Developing Elementary and Secondary School Programs.* Reston, VA: Council for Exceptional Children, 1975.

29. Bridges, S. *Problems of the Gifted Child: IQ 150.* New York: Crane Russak, 1974.

30. Butterfield, S.M., et al. *Developing IEPs for the Gifted/Talented.* Ventura, CA: National/State Leadership Training Institute on the Gifted and the Talented, Ventura County Superintendent of Schools, 1979.

31. Cox, R.L. "Background Characteristics of 456 Gifted Children." *Gifted Child Quarterly* 21, no. 2 (1977): 264.

32. *Creative Child and Adult Quarterly.* The National Association for Creative Children and Adults, 8080 Spring Valley Dr., Cincinnati, OH 45236. Quarterly. $22 nonmembers; $20 members.

33. Gallagher, James J. *Teaching the Gifted Child,* rev. ed. Boston: Allyn and Bacon, 1975.

34. Gallagher, James J., et al. *Issues in Gifted Education.* Ventura, CA: National/State Leadership Training Institute on the Gifted and the Talented, Ventura County Superintendent of Schools, 1979.

35. Goldberg, M.L. *How to Seek and How to Find Them: Identifying Gifted Pupils.* New York: Teachers College Press, Columbia University, 1974.

36. Gowan, J.C., and Bruch, C.B. *The Academically Talented and Guidance.* Boston: Houghton-Mifflin, 1977.

37. Gowan, J., Khatena, J., and Torrance, E., eds. *Educating the Ablest: A Book of Readings.* 2nd ed. Itasco, IL: Peacock, 1979.

38. Gowan, J., and Torrance, E.P. *Educating the Ablest.* Itasco, IL: Peacock, 1971.

39. Guilford, J.P. *Way Beyond the IQ.* Buffalo, NY: Creative Education Foundation, 1977.

40. Hagen, Elizabeth. *Identification of the Gifted.* New York: Teachers College Press, Columbia University, 1980.

41. Hauck, B., and Freehill, M. *The Gifted: Case Studies.* Dubuque, IA: W. C. Brown, 1972.

42. Hollingworth, L. *Children above 180 IQ Stanford Binet: Origins and Development.* New York: Arno, 1975.

43. Humphrey, N.K. "The Biological Basis of Collecting." *Human Nature* 2, no. 2 (Feb. 1979).

44. *The Journal for the Education of the Gifted.* The Association for the Gifted, 1920 Association Drive, Reston, VA 22091. Quarterly.

45. Lindsay, Margaret. *Training Teachers of the Gifted and Talented.* New York: Teachers College Press, Columbia University, 1980.

46. McGuinness, Diane. "How Schools Discriminate against Boys." *Human Nature* 2, no. 2 (Feb. 1979).

47. Martinson, R. *The Identification of the Gifted and Talented.* Ventura, CA: National/State Leadership Training Institute on the Gifted and the Talented, Ventura County Superintendent of Schools, 1973.

48. Means, Russell. "Fighting Words on the Future of the Earth." *Mother Jones*, December, 1980.

49. Miley, J., et al. *Promising Practices: Teaching the Disadvantaged Gifted.* Ventura, CA: National/State Leadership Training Institute on the Gifted and the Talented, Ventura County Superintendent of Schools, 1975.

50. Morgan, H.J., Tennant, C.G., and Gold, M.J. *Elementary and Secondary Level Programs for the Gifted and Talented.* New York: Teachers College Press, Columbia University, 1980.

51. Renzulli, J. *The Enrichment Triad Model: A Guide for Developing Defensible Programs for the Gifted and Talented.* Mansfield Center, CT: Creative Learning Press, 1977.

52. Renzulli, J., and Smith, L. *A Guidebook for Developing Individualized Programs for Gifted and Talented Students.* Mansfield Center, CT: Creative Learning Press, 1979.

53. Reynolds, M., ed. *Early School Admission for Mentally Advanced Children.* Reston, VA: Council for Exceptional Children, 1962.

54. Roedell, W.C., Jackson, N.E., and Robinson, H.B. *Gifted Young Children.* New York: Teachers College Press, Columbia University, 1980.

55. *Roeper Review: A Journal on Gifted Child Education.* Roeper City and County School, 2190 North Woodward, Bloomfield Hills, MI 48013.

56. Seagoe, M.V. *Terman and the Gifted.* Los Altos, CA: William Kaufmann.

57. Syphers, D. *Gifted and Talented: Practical Programming for Teachers and Principals.* Reston, VA: Council for Exceptional Children, 1972.

58. Torrance, E.P. *Discovery and Nurturance of Giftedness in the Culturally Different.* Reston, VA: Council for Exceptional Children, 1977.

59. Wooster, J. *What to Do for the Gifted Few.* Buffalo, NY: Disseminators of Knowledge, 1978.

# LEVEL C

60. Anastasi, Anne. *Psychological Testing.* New York: McMillan Company, 1961.

61. Arieti, S. *Creativity: The Magic Synthesis.* New York: Basic Books, 1976.

62. Ashley, R.M. *Activities for Motivating and Teaching Bright Children.* New York: Parker (Prentice Hall), 1973.

63. Bandura, Albert. *Principles of Behavior Modification.* New York: Holt, Rinehart & Winston, 1969.

64. Barbe, W.B., and Renzulli, J.S. *Psychology and Education of the Gifted*, 2nd ed. New York: Halsted Press, 1975.

65. Barron, F. *Creative Person and Creative Process.* New York: Holt, Rhinehart & Winston, 1969.

66. Biondi, A., and Parnes, S. *Assessing Creative Growth.* 2 vols. Great Neck, N.Y: Synergetic Assn., 1976.

67. Birnbaum, M. *Ideas for Urban/Rural Gifted/Talented Case Histories and Program Plans.* Ventura, CA: National/State Leadership Training Institute on the Gifted and the Talented, Ventura County Superintendent of Schools, 1977.

68. Bloom, Benjamin. *Taxonomy of Educational Objectives, Handbook I: Cognitive Domain.* New York: David McKay, 1956.

69. Clark, Barbara. *Growing Up Gifted.* Columbus, OH: Charles Merrill, 1979.

70. Clendening, Corinne P., and Davies, Ruth Ann. *Creating Programs for the Gifted: A Guide for Teachers, Librarians, and Students.* New York: R. R. Bowker, 1980.

71. Feldhusen, J., and Treffinger, D. *Teaching Creative Thinking and Problem Solving.* Dubuque, IA: Kendall-Hunt, 1976.

72. Fitzgerald, E., et al. *The First National Conference on the Disadvantaged Gifted.* Ventura, CA: National/State Leadership Training Institute on the Gifted and the Talented, Ventura County Superintendent of Schools, 1975.

73. Frederickson, R., and Rothney, J. *Recognizing and Assisting Multipotential Youth.* Columbus, OH: Charles Merrill, 1972.

74. Gallagher, James J. *Research Summary on Gifted Child Education.* Springfield, IL: State of Illinois, 1966.

75. *The Gifted Child Quarterly.* National Association for Gifted Children, 217 Gregory Dr., Hot Springs, AR 71901. Free to members.

76. Gilmore, John V. *The Productive Personality.* San Francisco: Albion Publishing Co., 1974.

77. Goertzel, V., and Goertzel, M. *Cradles of Eminence.* Boston: Little, Brown, 1978.

78. Guilford, J.P. *The Nature of Human Intelligence.* New York: McGraw-Hill, 1967.

79. Johnson, Barbara, ed. *Advantage: Disadvantaged Gifted, Presentations from the Third National Conference on Disadvantaged Gifted.* Ventura, CA: National/State Leadership Training Institute on the Gifted and the Talented, Ventura County Superintendent of Schools, 1975.

80. Johnson, Barbara, ed. *Ideas for Urban/Rural Gifted/Talented: Case History and Program Plans.* Ventura, CA: National/State Leadership Training Institute on the Gifted and the Talented, Ventura County Superintendent of Schools, 1975.

81. *The Journal of Creative Behavior.* The Creative Education Foundation, State University College at Buffalo, 1300 Elmwood Ave., Buffalo, NY 14222. Quarterly. $10.

82. Keating, Daniel P. *Intellectual Talent: Research and Development.* Baltimore, MD: The Johns Hopkins University Press, 1976.

83. Laycock, F. *Gifted Children.* Glenview, IL: Scott, Foresman, 1979.

84. McCurdy, Harold G. "Childhood Patterns of Genius." In *Advanced Intellectual Assessment: Readings in Theory and Application*, edited by H. Kassinove, M. Meier, and J. Vane, New York: Selected Academic Readings, Division of Associated Educational Services, 1969, pp. 448–462.

85. Maker, J. *Training Teachers for the Gifted and Talented: A Comparison of Models.* Reston, VA: Council for Exceptional Children, 1975.

86. Maker, J. *Providing Programs for the Gifted Handicapped.* Reston, VA: Council for Exceptional Children, 1977.

87. Marland, Sidney. *Education of the Gifted and Talented.* (Report to the Congress of the United States by the U.S. Commissioner of Education). 2 vols. Washington, DC: U.S. Government Printing Office, 1972.

88. Martinson, R. *A Guide toward Better Teaching for the Gifted.* Ventura, CA: National/State Leadership Training Institute on the Gifted and the Talented, Ventura County Superintendent of Schools, 1976.

89. Martinson, R. *Curriculum Enrichment for the Gifted in the Primary Grades.* Englewood Cliffs, NJ: Prentice-Hall, 1968.

90. Meeker, Mary. *Advance Teaching Judgment, Planning and Decision Making.* SOI Institute (214 Main St., El Segundo, CA 90245), 1976.

91. Meeker, Mary. *The Structure of Intellect: Its Interpretation and Uses.* Columbus, OH: Charles Merrill, 1969.

92. Parnes, S., Noller, Ruth, and Biondi, A. *Guide to Creative Action*, rev. ed. New York: Scribner's, 1977.

93. Pegnato, C., and Birch, J. "Locating Gifted Children in Junior High Schools: A Comparison of Methods." *Exceptional Children* 25 (1959): 300–304.

94. Renzulli, J.S., and Hartman, R.K. "Scale for Rating Behavioral Characteristics of Superior Students." *Exceptional Children* 38, no. 3 (1971): 243–248.

95. Rothenberg, A., and Hausman, C.R., eds. *The Creativity Question.* Durham, NC: Duke University Press, 1976.

96. Stanley, J.C., George, W.C., and Solano, C.H., eds. *Educational Programs and Intellectual Prodigies.* Baltimore, MD: The Johns Hopkins University Press, 1978.

97. Stanley, J.C., Keating, D.P., and Fox, Lynn. *Mathematical Talent: Discovery, Description and Development.* Baltimore, MD: The Johns Hopkins University Press, 1974.

98. Stanley, J.C., George, W.C., and Solano, C.H., eds. *The Gifted and the Creative: A Fifty Year Perspective.* Baltimore, MD: The Johns Hopkins University Press, 1978.

99. Torrance, E. P., and Myers, R. E. *Creative Learning and Teaching.* New York: Dodd, Mead, 1970.

100. Wechsler, David. *Manual for the Wechsler Intelligence Scale for Children—Revised.* New York: The Psychological Corporation, 1974.

101. Wechsler, David. *Manual for the Wechsler Preschool and Primary Scale of Intelligence.* New York: The Psychological Corporation, 1967.

102. Whitmore, J.R. *Giftedness, Conflict and Underachievement.* Boston: Allyn and Bacon, 1980.

103. Williams, Frank E. "Assessing Creativity Across Williams' Cube Model." *Gifted Child Quarterly* 23, no. 4 (Winter 1979): 748–756.

104. Ziv, A. *Counseling the Intellectually Gifted.* New York: Teachers College Press, Columbia University, 1977.

# Index